Col. James W. Starnes commanding "Forrest's Old Brigade" (2n
in Forrest's Cavalry Division, 1863

FORREST'S FORGOTTEN HORSE BRIGADIER

—ILLUSTRATED—

H. Gerald Starnes

HERITAGE BOOKS
2009

HERITAGE BOOKS

AN IMPRINT OF HERITAGE BOOKS, INC.

Books, CDs, and more—Worldwide

For our listing of thousands of titles see our website
at
www.HeritageBooks.com

Published 2009 by
HERITAGE BOOKS, INC.
Publishing Division
100 Railroad Ave. #104
Westminster, Maryland 21157

International Standard Book Numbers
Paperbound: 978-0-7884-0234-0
Clothbound: 978-0-7884-8282-3

Dedication

*To Mrs. Virginia M. Bowman, Williamson County, Tennessee
Historian and to
Mrs. Mary Starnes DeMoss, Great-granddaughter of Col.
James W. Starnes*

Acknowledgement

*To Wanda Starnes Argiropoulos for Editing and Proofreading
and to
Herman Starnes for assistance in researching court records*

Preface

Numerous books and probably hundreds of articles have been published about the military genius and the absolute fearlessness exhibited by Nathan Bedford Forrest during the Civil War. While the bravery and tactical instincts of General Forrest in combat are beyond question, there is a discernible absence of mention or information on the sub-commanders who executed the general's strategies and orders in many of these biographical volumes and articles. Most of these literary efforts were well written, well researched, and are historically accurate. But for the knowledge of military command, much of the narrative of the battles would leave the novice reader with the impression that the general was the only officer in the field and that he personally issued every directive. It is interesting to note that in Forrest's December 1862 raid into West Tennessee, everyone of his regimental commanders were ordered out alone to accomplish specific objectives, and all of them performed capably at independent command.

When the Starnes family history and genealogy was published in 1984, inquiries were received from students and history buffs of the War Between the States, who had expected to find information on Col. James W. Starnes in this large volume. Nothing was known about the man other than bits of his wartime exploits, which had been published in the O.R., and books and pieces written about General Forrest. No descendants could be found and none of his kin could be located in Williamson County, Tennessee where, in 1861, he had raised and drilled a company of cavalry.

The prominence of this physician turned cavalry leader during the early years of the war, and the apparent obliviousness that followed, created a curiosity that quickly led us to Williamson County, Tennessee. Careful study of almost a century of Starnes family court records, that began about 1820 and ended suddenly in 1912, revealed many facts concerning the forgotten Dr. James W. Starnes. The Starnes and Rudder cemeteries and former plantation lands were located and visited. A reenactment of the Battle of Parker's Crossroads was attended and discussions were held with anyone having any interest in, or information about, the Confederate Cavalry hero, Col. Starnes. Local library sources were also perused for a few more informational morsels.

Our research efforts were most fortunate in our making the acquaintance of the Williamson County Historian, who has so generously shared her extensive knowledge of regional history, and of this particular family's history and that of other families to which they were related. Through her helpful endeavors, we have been in contact with the great-grandchildren of James W. and Mary C. Rudder Starnes, who have become very interested in learning about their famous ancestor. They have been both cooperative and helpful in every way they were able.

A rather fascinating story slowly emerged as the details about the man, James W. Starnes, were pieced together in chronological order. It was indeed a colorful narrative about antebellum life, and the war that came quickly to the Middle Tennessee region of the Old South.

After serving as a regimental surgeon in the Mexican War, Dr. Starnes, like his father before him, practiced medicine and operated a plantation on the Harpeth River. He gave up his practice, ostensibly to allow him to better manage the plantations. But it is interesting to note, that this decision followed the death of his first two children, whom he could not save.

When secession and war appeared imminent, rather than serve again as a physician, Starnes chose cavalry command as his contribution to the cause, and began organizing a company of mounted men. In his first combat action in Kentucky, he earned the respect and friendship of the then unknown former slave trader from Memphis, Nathan Bedford Forrest.

Forrest and Starnes had in common a total disregard for their own personal safety, and a eager willingness to fight even though seriously outnumbered. Otherwise, the contrast in their personalities and demeanor showed striking differences. General Forrest was a man of large stature who had almost no formal schooling. Col. Starnes had a smaller than average frame, and was very well educated. "Old Bedford" was noted for shouting obscenities, and yelling at those in his command; while the little Colonel politely and quietly gave orders to his men, and often asked them to perform some important actions on the field of battle. However, their joint effectiveness in the chain of command was beyond repute.

Accounts of the near disaster at Parker's Crossroads, where Forrest's Brigade was surprised and caught between two Federal Brigades, have rather implied that Col. Starnes, and Capt. W. S. McLemore, were derelict in the performance of their orders to guard the rear of the brigade. If this were the case, given the personality of General Forrest, why was Starnes promoted to command Forrest's Old Brigade, and McLemore promoted to the command of Starnes' Cavalry? It was another credit to Forrest for acknowledging the ambiguousness of his written orders; that they had been interpreted to direct a reconnaissance to the rear, and not the posting of a strong rear guard.

Forrest expected the capability of quick and independent action by his sub-commanders when an unexpected ambush or attack occurred. During the April, 1863 Confederate attack on Franklin, Tennessee, Starnes had counterattacked and routed the 8th U. S. Cavalry when they fell on his flank and surprised his brigade (who had not yet loaded their arms) by the time General Forrest arrived on the scene. Mutual goodwill and admiration continued between these two cavalry leaders until the Colonel's untimely death in front of Tullahoma in mid-1863. The war continued for almost two years, and the third most famous Tennessee cavalryman was forgotten.

CONTENTS

ILLUSTRATIONS

Illustrations

Maps

A Kentucky Line of Defense

Riding out of Russellville in the Saturday morning winter chill of December 28, 1861, a company of some forty Tennessee cavalry overtook a detachment of their Confederate brethren under the command of a Lt. Col. N.B. Forrest on the icy, dirt road north of Greenville, Kentucky. This band of horsemen, from the 8th Battalion, Tennessee Cavalry, called themselves the " Williamson County Cavalry." They were commanded by Lt. Col. James W. Starnes, a prominent county physician and planter-turned-horse soldier, and Capt. William S. McLemore, the court clerk from the Middle Tennessee county of that name. Sometime before Tennesseans had reversed their option in a second vote in June 1861, thereby overwhelmingly electing to secede, this small group of southern stalwarts had begun to organize and drill in McGavock's Grove. This field was near "Carnton," the McGavock Mansion that, some three years later, was to play a significant role in the Battle of Franklin.

At South Carrolltown, Kentucky the day before, Starnes' men had had their first encounter with Union cavalry and claimed to have killed three. That cold night two days after Christmas, Starnes rode into the Muhlenberg County courthouse where a detachment of Forrest's Cavalry Battalion was just finishing supper, "a royal feast," as guests of the "good people" of Greenville. He informed their commanding officer, a former Alabamian parson, Maj. David C. Kelly, that a Federal scouting party was out. The dinner party came to an abrupt end as pickets were sent out and the Rebel cavalry prepared to fight, if they didn't freeze to death before the Yankees arrived.

Starnes' company voluntarily agreed to join Forrest's troopers who were making an observation of enemy strength toward Henderson, Kentucky (a border state) on orders from Brig. Gen. Charles Clark. On their own, they were looking for a fight to prove their mettle.

The Tennessee legislature had authorized the raising and equipping of 55,000 troops for the Provisional Army of Tennessee, May 15, 1861. By the end of July, Governor Isham G. Harris began turning over more than 100,000 men to the Confederacy. On October 30th in Nashville, this company of Williamson County Cavalry was mustered into Confederate service. Now they were in Kentucky along with other widely dispersed and untried military organizations. Their newly assigned commander of the western army, Gen. Albert Sydney Johnston, was trying to establish a line of defense across the state from Columbus to Bowling Green and the Cumberland Gap.

It was a desperate southern hope that Kentucky would soon join the Confederacy. The occupation of Columbus and closing off of transportation on the lower Mississippi had, in reality, already ended any chance that Kentucky would form a political alliance with the cause of secession.

In the afternoon a scout reported an estimated 500 Federal cavalry (the Official Record states 168) about eight miles ahead. Forrest determined to overtake and attack this force. As they neared the village of Sacramento, a Kentucky belle, her long tresses floating on the winter air and mounted on a magnificent animal, appeared from nowhere to gallop along with the officers and men, urging them on. About a mile out of the village, the Union cavalry rear guard was sighted, and a chase was on right through the little settlement and up the road to a grove of trees. Here the officers of this pursued detachment of Col. James C. Jackson's 3rd Kentucky Cavalry Regiment, U.S. Volunteers under the command of Maj. Eli Murray, decided to make a stand.

This was Forrest's first real fight. He formed a skirmish line to hold the attention of the Federals, then sent Lt. Col. Starnes, who had rushed up from the rear guard position, to the left, and Maj. D.C. Kelly to the right, to execute his famous "by the flank and rear movement."

When Starnes and Kelly got into position to disturb the Union cavalry by threatening their flanks, Forrest ordered his men to charge without regard to military formation. This charge of over 200 Confederates took on all the aspects of a mud-spattering horse race up the now thawed Rumsey Road. The best mounted rebels, Starnes, Forrest and Capt. C.E. "Ned" Merriwether, a Kentuckian who couldn't let Tennesseans outride him in his home state, outran their troops and rode into a group of the fleeing cavalry that the Union officers had rallied to meet the charge. The studious and cautious Maj. Kelly thought that his commander, and Starnes and Merriwether, had lost their senses in their eagerness to fight. By that time they had been at the gallop for most of eight miles.

Merriwether, riding just behind Forrest, was killed by a pistol shot through the head. Forrest mortally wounded Capt A.G. Bacon with a left hand saber thrust. Pvt. William H. Terry, a close neighbor of Starnes and a member of his company, spurring his horse to Forrest's side, received a fatal saber thrust from Capt. A.N. Davis. Forrest then collided with Davis, and both horses and men went down in a heap on the road as other horses and men fell over them. Capt. Davis' shoulder was dislocated and he was taken prisoner.

Meanwhile Lt. Col. Starnes found himself at the head of this mad rush and into a battle of his own on the road just ahead of the pileup of men and horses. As the Federals disengaged and retreated up the road, Starnes, who fired with either hand, threw his empty pistol at his departing Union adversary which, striking the man in the back, only helped to send him on his way.

It was said that Lt. Col. Starnes killed two men in this encounter. He received a saber cut on the head and one on each shoulder. None of these were serious wounds.

"Carnton"

The Rear Veranda; further to the rear of the house Capt. James W. S Starnes drilled his company of Williamson County Tennessee Cavalry

(The bodies of four Confederate Generals lay on this veranda after the Battle of Franklin, November 30, 1864)

FORM No 3-Officer's Pay Account.

The Confederate States of America, *To* Cbh Jas M Flann Dr.

ON WHAT ACCOUNT.	Commencement and Expiration.		Term of service charged.		Pay per month.		Amount.		Remarks.
	From—	To—	Months.	Days.	Dolls.	Cts.	Dolls.	Cts.	
Pay—									
For myself	October 30th	December 11th	1	12	140	—	196		
For	year's service								
Forage for	horses						$		

I hereby certify that the foregoing account is accurate and just; that I have not been absent without leave during any part of the time charged for; that I have not received pay, forage, or received money in lieu of any part thereof, for any part of the time therein charged; that the horses were actually kept in service and were mustered for the whole of the time charged; that for the whole of the time charged for my staff appointment, I actually and legally held the appointment and did duty in the department; that I have been a commissioned officer for the number of years stated in the charge for every additional five years service; that I am not in arrears with the Confederate States, on any account whatsoever; and that the last payment received was from........... *Mr.* .... *Q. M. ....* ...., 186:.

....to the .... day of ...., 186:.

I, at the same, acknowledge that I have received of .... *N F Madders etc.* .... *Q M Clay*, ...

this .... day of ...., 186-, the sum of .... *One Hundred* ....

.... *Ninety Six* .... 100 dollars, being the amount, in full, of said account.

Pay........ $ 196

To........ year's service........

Forage........

Amount— $ 196

[Signed Duplicates.]

Chs W Flann B Capt
Tenn Cavalry

The 8th Battalion of Tennessee Cavalry had been organized at Camp Cheatham in Robertson County on December 11, 1861, with James W. Starnes commissioned Lieutenant Colonel to command it. The original company of Williamson County Cavalry was designated Company "F" in the battalion. This company, recruited by Starnes in the vicinity of Franklin, Tennessee, was described by one of its members as a choice body of troopers, most of whom came from families of wealth, position and culture. The command was almost entirely armed with double-barreled, muzzle-loading shotguns, a situation that was to frustrate the former physician for months.

With this impetuous charge into Union cavalry, seemingly unmindful of personal risk in his first combat action, Starnes' reputation as a fighting leader of southern horse soldiers had its beginning. And it also began a personal friendship and mutual respect, between Nathan Bedford Forrest and himself, that lasted until the Tullahoma Campaign, over a year and a half later.

On New Year's Day, 1862, four days after the action at Sacramento, Starnes requested sabers for his men. Capt. McLemore was to comment years later that this was the only fight in which he recalled ever having seen sabers used as weapons in combat during the war.

Still at Russelville, Starnes sent another urgent request for pistols and sabers on January 31, 1862 to Capt. Moses H. Wright, ordinance stores officer for Maj. Gen. Leonidas Polk. He enclosed a blank requisition and pleaded for "pistols and sabers, whatever you may have on hand."

Dr. James W. Starnes was a graduate of the Jefferson Seminary Medical School (later the University of Louisville). The doctor was 43 years old when he entered Confederate service. With the inheritance of his wife, Mary Christine Rudder, and his own holdings, they owned over 1,000 acres on the south side of the Harpeth River and about forty slaves. The business of managing the farms had become so demanding that he had given up the practice of medicine to devote all his time to the southern agrarian economy. Starnes also had a large cotton plantation near Friar's Point in the river bottom in Mississippi.

The eldest of ten children of physician-planter, Dr. Samuel Scott Starnes and Nancy Matilda Wellborn Starnes, James W. was born at the home of his maternal grandparents on July 9, 1817 in Wilkes County, North Carolina. Shortly thereafter his parents moved from Augusta, Georgia to Tennessee. The boy grew up under the traditional guidance and training of his parents to be master of the tract of land on the north bank of the Harpeth River once known as "Commissioners Trace." A rather handsome man of smaller than average stature, he seemed to possess all the cultural and social graces expected of him.

Gentle, tender hands and a polite, assuring bedside manner endeared the young doctor to his patients. Upon the death of both of his parents within a year, James, in his twenties, assumed the medical practice of his father (affectionately known in the area as "Uncle Doctor") and the guardianship of six minor siblings. He also discreetly and slightly changed his middle name, Wellborn (his mother's maiden name), to Wilburn.

During the Mexican War in 1846, young Dr. Starnes reported for duty in Memphis as Assistant Regimental Surgeon of the 1st Tennessee Infantry, with his right arm in a sling. It seems he and a Mr. Hill, who lived in the old, brick Crockett house near the doctor's aunt, had an unknown personal disagreement between them, which was believed to be a land boundary dispute involving the doctor's father's plantation. One day the two met unexpectedly on a narrow lane near Hill's home at Arrington, Tennessee.

Hill attacked the doctor with a heavy, hickory stick, knocking him from his horse and breaking his right arm which had been raised to protect his head. Before Starnes could rise, Hill jumped from his mount and continued the attack by striking his victim several times over the head. Starnes came up with a large knife in his left hand and seriously wounded his assailant, who ran for his house, crossing two rail fences, with the doctor in pursuit. Hill locked his door, neighbors came out and took the doctor to his aunt's home

Russellville Ky
Jany 31st 1862

Capt M H Wright
                    Sir
                              Inclosed
I send you the receipt for articles
forwarded to me —
           My Battalion is in great need
of Pistols & Sabers, doing a goodeel
of Scouting and always when out of
comeing in conflict with greatly superior
Numbers. Please let me have of pistols
and sabers whatever you may have
on hand. Cpt Robb has wagons that
are comeing here and will take charge
of them —
           Inclosed you will find a
blank requisition. There is due me
480 Sabers Belts & plate — and pistols
           very respectfully &c
                    Jas W Harris Lt Col
              Com g 8t Batt Ten Cavalry

where a visiting physician, Dr. Richardson from Rutherford County, the husband of one of Dr. Starnes' cousins, skillfully set his broken arm and tended his other injuries. Cousin John E. Tulloss rode to Memphis with Dr. Starnes where he boarded a boat for Mexico.

Mr. Hill was disabled for several months. When he was able, the gentleman went before the circuit court judge in Franklin and stated that had he not made an attack, there would not have been a fight.

In northern Mexico Dr. Starnes taught himself to fire a pistol with his left hand as accurately as he had previously been able to fire with the injured right arm that was still in a sling. When the regimental surgeon, Dr. Daniel McPhail, died at Camargo, "the graveyard," Starnes was promoted to that position (which was equivalent to the rank of Captain) by the regimental commander, Col. William B. Campbell, who later refused high Confederate rank to become Brigadier General, U.S. Volunteers.

Though surgeons are not expected to engage in combat, Starnes fought in the lines alongside the infantrymen of John A. Quitman's Brigade, where Maj. Braxton Bragg commanded the artillery and Col. Jefferson Davis the regiment of mounted Mississippi Rifles.

On February 6th, just south of the Kentucky state line, occurred the capture of the closed, fieldwork-mounting of 17 guns of Fort Henry on the low ground on the Tennessee River. Ten days later, under siege at Fort Donelson on the Cumberland River, Brig. Gens. John B. Floyd and Gideon Pillow turned over command to Brig. Gen. Simon B. Buckner and fled toward Nashville. Bruckner surrendered unconditionally to his friend since West Point days, Brig. Gen. U.S. Grant. All of these generals had served with Lt. Col. Starnes in the Mexican War.

Monday morning February 17th, a crowd of excited and distraught citizens of the city of Nashville rushed down to meet the river steamboat coming up the Cumberland to the landing. Floyd and Pillow disembarked and went to see Gen. A.S. Johnston, who was preparing to depart without a fight before the surrender of the city, much to the dismay of Mayor R.B. Cheatham and the majority of the people. Johnston placed Floyd in command. Some 1,500 of his men, portions of his Virginia regiments and others who evaded capture, had straggled into Nashville over muddy roads during a period of drenching downpours. Pillow left for his home in Columbia, Tennessee.

By Tuesday morning at 10 AM, there was a state of absolute chaos and near riot as the contents of government warehouses were being distributed, when Col. Forrest's regiment of cavalry clattered into the streets of the capital from their escape at Fort Donelson. Floyd turned over command to Forrest, who saw the hysteria and used his troops as military police to forcefully impose some order and to impress labor to move military stores.

As Forrest continued to move military stores as fast as he could, sometime the next day, Starnes' Battalion rode into the wild scene in Nashville. Normally, crowds would have cheered at the arrival of the fully intact, veteran, cavalry organizations of Forrest and Starnes as the defenders of their city. Starnes' men drew what supplies and rations they could get from the warehouses among the chaos of other units trying to do the same thing. They stayed only one day, then rode out toward Gen. Johnston's muddy, demoralized assembly of troops at Murfreesboro, who had been forced to retreat from Donelson and Kentucky. The battalion made camp out on the Nolensville Pike, just south of the settlement.

That day Nashville became the first capital of a southern state to be occupied by Union forces, February 24, 1862. Gen. Johnston ordered Gen. Floyd to take command of Starnes's Battalion and march with them to Chattanooga. A few days later, as Floyd's motley brigade of Donelson survivors and assigned cavalry moved out of the Murfreesboro encampment, retreating towards Chattanooga, Starnes' Battalion served as the rear guard. Gen. Floyd's disheartened men were inclined to straggle and fall out of the line of march anywhere they could. Starnes used his cavalry to keep them up and moving until they reached Chattanooga.

The View Looking towards the City of Monterrey, Mexico and "Saddle Notch" from the Bishop's Palace on Obispado Hill. 1st Tennessee Infantry Regimental Surgeon, Dr. J.W. Starnes fought in the distant extreme left near the present higher buildings.

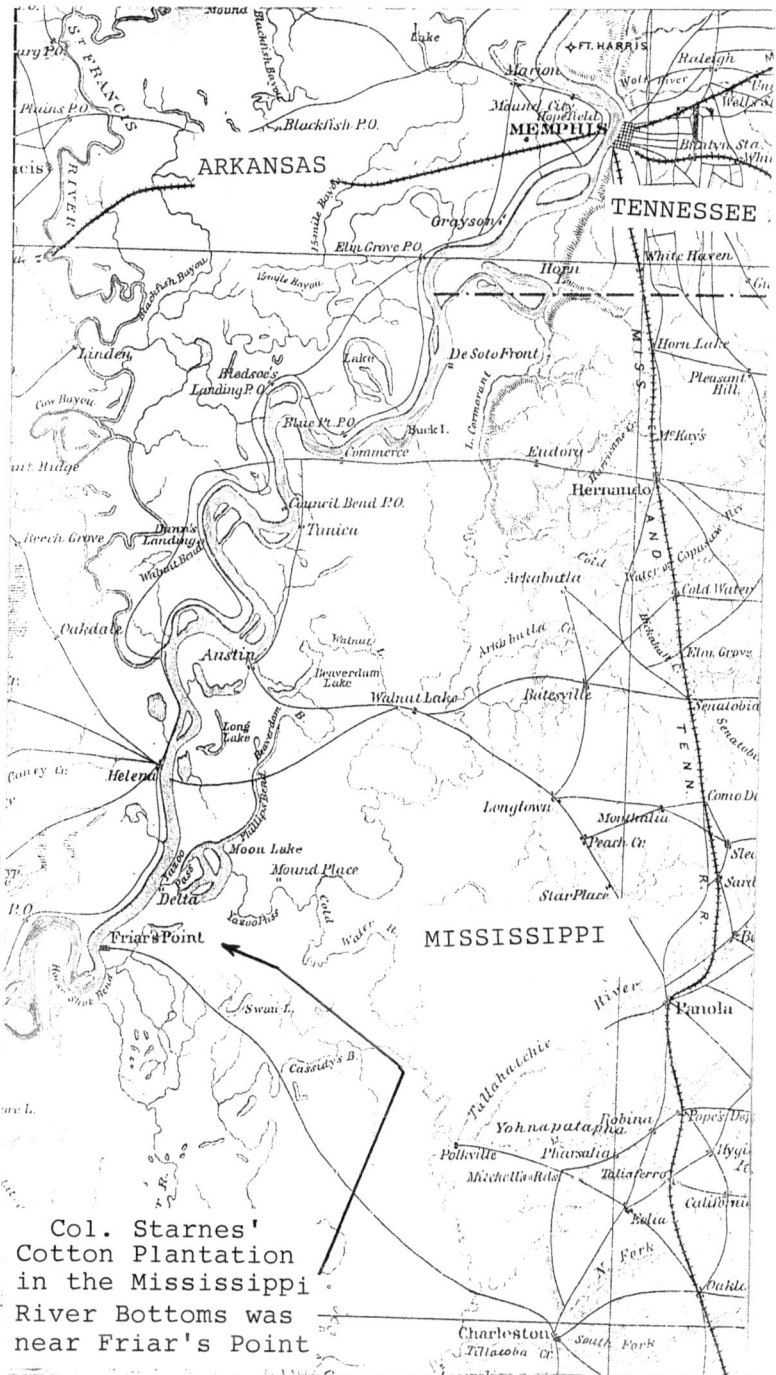

Col. Starnes'
Cotton Plantation
in the Mississippi
River Bottoms was
near Friar's Point

Scouting and Skirmishing in East Tennessee

Operating in the eastern part of Tennessee, poorly armed and under Gen. Floyd, was not to Starnes' liking:

Chattanooga [March] 13th 1862

Gen. Johnston

The officers and privates of 9th Battalion Tennessee Cavalry most respectfully petition you to have us ordered to the middle or western part of Tennessee where we may have an opportunity of getting into active service. Genl. Floyd now having as many cavalry as infantry accessions made to Col. [E.S.] Smith's Battalion is now ordered into Regt with the very poor appreciation Gen Floyd has of cavalry not having opportunity of knowing the effectiveness of my command. We think that the efficiency of our battalion will be very materially injured under his command & East Tennessee for which reason we make this petition It is true we are poorly armed but if you will give us the opportunity of getting near the enemy we will arm ourselves we have thus far conducted ourselves with great circumspection towards citizens and conformed to army regulations and expect ever to do the same as Gentlemen and soldiers the only object of this petition being to make ourselves most efficient for our bleeding country. Please answer

Your obedt. servant &C.

Jas. W. Starnes
Lt Col. commd'g

Two days before Starnes had written the above correspondence to Gen. A.S. Johnston on March 13, 1862 from Chattanooga, Pres. Jefferson Davis wrote to Judah P. Benjamin, Secretary of War, in Richmond. The President stated that the reports of Brigadier Generals Floyd and Pillow of the defense and fall of Fort Donelson were unsatisfactory, and directed the Secretary to order Gen. A. S. Johnston to relieve them of command.

At Chattanooga, Starnes' 8th Battalion came under the Confederate Department of East Tennessee commanded by Maj. Gen. E. Kirby Smith, who also reported it poorly armed. The battalion was also briefly referred to as the 9th Tennessee Cavalry Battalion. As the result of the rapid formation of military organizations and commands in 1861 and early 1862, the authorities did not always know the correct numerical order or the name of the commanding officer of a unit. Further confusion occurred when the state troops were accepted for Confederate service. Some dual, numerical designations lasted throughout the war and the commanding officers' names were used to differentiate between them.

While the depleted Confederate and reinforced Union western armies concentrated their forces near the Tennessee and Mississippi border for the Battle of Shiloh (April 6-8, 1862) and the Corinth Campaign (to June 10th), there was considerable scouting and skirmishing activity in the higher, eastern areas of Tennessee. The military importance of Chattanooga, as a vital communications, river and rail center, was obvious to both governments. Confederate forces in Chattanooga numbered barely over 2,000.

Starnes was sent out of Hillsboro with a detachment of his 8th Battalion, "for the purpose of scouring the country by near the western slopes of the Cumberland Mountains." He was determined to surprise and attack a much larger force than his own at Wartrace on the Nashville and Chattanooga Railroad. After an all night ride, they came upon the Federal encampment "about sun up," April 10, 1862. The plan was to attack dismounted. But in the execution of the order, Pvt. John Lee of Company "F " let his gun go off accidently. Momentary confusion reigned, then all the battalion, except about 30 men of Company "F" who had dismounted, charged on horseback, firing their shotguns at close range among the Yankees, who were quickly taking to their arms. Lt. Col. Starnes led the mounted charge and his men thought he was sure to be killed.

Lt. T.F.P. Allison commanding the men on foot, came up and attacked vigorously. Initially the Federals were driven back to a creek bed near their camp. But Allison's men were so few in numbers, they were forced to retreat uphill through a field of high clover, with casualties of at least one killed and several seriously wounded. Total casualties were reported as three killed and eight wounded.

On April 13th the battalion was ordered from Chattanooga to operate on the Nashville and Chattanooga road.

At Camp Robinson in the Sequatchie Valley on May 26, 1862, the battalion was increased to a regiment by adding Companies "G" and "H" from the 2nd (Col. E.S. Smith's) Tennessee and two newly organized companies. Company "I" was organized April 10th at Grahamville from various companies of the first organization of the 16th Tennessee Infantry Regiment.

Company "K" was organized of men from north Alabama and Franklin County, Tennessee on the day the regiment was formed. The original six companies of the battalion, "A" through "F," bore the same letters in the regiment.

Capt. W.C. Kain's Tennessee Light Artillery left Chattanooga for Winchester on May 29th to join Col. Starnes' new 3rd Regiment, Tennessee Cavalry,which was later officially designated as the 4th Regiment. At Altamont they caught up with Starnes.

About the first of June 1862 Col. Starnes crossed the Cumberland Mountains with 300 of his regiment, a section of two iron, four-pounder guns from Capt. Kain's battery, and 80 men under Maj. W.N. Estes (formerly of Col. E.S. Smith's Regt.). He had made arrangements with Col. John Adams, commanding a cavalry brigade, and Col. William G.M. Davis, commanding a Florida infantry brigade, to join him some four miles from the Cowan Depot.

Upon arriving at the designated point, Starnes found an enemy force, that he estimated at 4,500, passing up the mountain. He believed he could form a junction with Colonels Adams and Davis at Jasper before the Federals could arrive there.

The advance units of this Federal expedition of infantry, cavalry and artillery left Fayetteville under the command of Brig. Gen. James S. Negley on June 1st. On the 2nd they entered Winchester and drove out the Confederate cavalry, which they reported to be "under Starnes." The column was headed for Jasper where, it was hoped, the Rebels would underestimate their strength (about 6,000) and make a stand.

Like Forrest, Starnes wasn't very much concerned about attacking a force considerably larger than his own if an opportunity were presented. But Negley's force was far too much for him as he hung on its flank and skirmished for two days, hoping to join forces with Adams and Davis for an attack. Recrossing the mountain to Tracy City, he learned that the enemy was already in possession of Jasper and that his command would be cut off before he could possibly reach Chattanooga. The colonel then decided to head north for McMinville by way of Altamont. On June 6th he sent a message from ten miles north of Winchester to department headquarters in Knoxville: "2, 000 abolitionists advancing from McMinville on Chattanooga."

In camp 15 miles from McMinville, Col. Starnes learned that Union cavalry had dashed into town and captured most of his men in Company "F," who had had permission to get their saddles repaired, and immediately moved forward to attack them with 100 volunteers formed into three companies. He didn't overtake these "Abolitionists," as the colonel was prone to call all Federals, until daylight on the morning of June 7th, after an all-night ride. This was at a place called Readyville, some 27 miles beyond McMinville.

This Union scouting detail, consisting of a major and 100 men, was at breakfast when Pvts. J.R. Harris, an Alabamian from "F" company, and William M. Whitworth from company "K," who had been in the lead, captured the picket in front of Burton House. Before the main body of the troops could come up, a negro boy discovered those two rebels and ran around the house shouting an alarm. There were about thirty men in the house, and they rushed to the front and began firing. Whitworth fired a double-barrelled load of buckshot from the side of the house into the dining room, from which came cries of "We surrender," as other troopers came up with their shotguns.

Most of the command charged the large, brick Ready House. When the troopers at the Burton House looked up from taking the surrender there, some of them made their way through a field of rye and got very near the rear of Ready House before being discovered. Rebel losses were two horses killed and a few men wounded, none seriously.

In that fight, Starnes' companies killed eight and captured 54 from a Pennsylvania and a Kentucky regiment, and 14 from the bodyguards of Pres. Lincoln's appointed military Governor of Tennessee, Andrew Johnson. The only expedient thing the colonel could do was to parole the captives, which he did on the Sparta road. In the report, Starnes sought to bring to the notice of the commanding general, a Pvt. W.F. Whittsitt, who killed three of the enemy with one shot and a fourth with the other barrel of his shotgun. Some of the "Marshall (County) Rangers," who had just transferred into Starnes' Regiment in May, summed up their first real fight under the little colonel as, "69 Yankees captured and a few killed."

That weekend of June 7-8, 1862, the Federal expedition reached Chattanooga in force and made an attack. There was some artillery dueling, but the efforts of the Union forces were, in reality, more of a serious demonstration. Gen. Negley did not consider the capture and holding of the place very difficult or hazardous if they were prepared to do so. However, he considered the exposed condition that their front and rear lines would be in. And further, he had to be concerned with the long lines of communication and supply that would stretch all the way back to Pittsburg Landing on the Tennessee River.

Negley made another demonstration Sunday morning against the city, while starting his trains down the mountain. He retired his forces by different routes, "so as to drive Starnes to Knoxville." At midnight June 10th, according to Federal reports, a party of about 200 of Starnes' cavalry captured a cotton and sutlers train on the Fayetteville road about 16 miles north of the Division Headquarters of Maj. Gen. O.M. Mitchell in Huntsville, Tennessee. Col. J.C. Walker (35th Indiana Infantry) reported Starnes' cavalry as "about 1,600 strong in the vicinity of Pelham," Tennessee on June 12th. Starnes was in Loudon on the upper Tennessee River, about 30 miles southwest of Knoxville, when he wrote his report June 16th.

Orders from Knoxville were being issued thick and fast as Kirby Smith was preparing to invade Kentucky. On the 17th a dispatch advised the commander of the post in Kingston that "Starnes will remain with you." That same day he was ordered to move his headquarters to Cleveland, and move his command to observe that neighborhood, back to the Chattanooga area. (Kirby Smith was considering his retreat route via Cleveland and into Georgia, should he not win a large and decisive battle in the Bluegrass State.) The following day, June 18th, in response to a report of a body of enemy moving between the Clinch River and Walden's Ridge, a message to the commanding officer at Loudon, Tennessee stated, "After Starnes has rested and recruited his command, direct him to look out for them."

Sunday was no day of rest. June 22nd brought orders from Gen. Smith to Loudon: "Send up Starnes' cavalry without delay." Col. Starnes, on the road toward Kingston, received orders to push on with all dispatch with his cavalry to Knoxville and, immediately on arrival, report to the General in person. Monday brought yet another directive to the colonel: to move with the least possible delay to Maynardville and "throw forward his cavalry to keep back the enemy cavalry from foraging around the country." While on the march, his instructions were modified to move to Blain's Crossroads and communicate with the major commanding at Maynardville, and govern himself by such orders or information as he may receive.

If Starnes wasn't in the mood to return to Middle Tennessee, Monday's dispatch of orders from Kirby Smith would certainly have placed the thought in his mind. Smith sent a dispatch to Brig. Gen. Carter L. Stevenson commanding the Second Brigade: "I think I shall order Colonel Starnes to Rogersville to scout in Hawkins and Hancock." These two counties were well known for Union sympathies, which caused Smith to remind Stevenson that Starnes' command is from Middle Tennessee, and he suggested that if Capt. Frank I. Phipps' newly organized company of Partisan Rangers could be found, they might be ordered to report to Col. Starnes and act as guides for him. This Partisan Ranger company had been organized May 24, 1862 at Lyons Store in Hawkins County. Starnes' orders were to move his command to Rogersville via Bean's Station. At Bean's Station he was to report to Stevenson for any possible instructions. He was to scout toward Estillville, Virginia, watch the enemy at Cumberland Gap, and drive back any incursion into the Clinch Valley. Furthermore, he was advised that he could not operate successfully with wagons in that terrain, would draw his supplies from the country, and was to send all his wagons, except two, to Knoxville.

With Union headquarters in the transportation and communications center of Nashville, and with intense sympathies for the Confederacy, the place became a natural center for smuggling and espionage. As late as the first of June 1862, substantial shipments made their way into rebel lines. One thousand pairs of shoes from Nashville were reported to have been delivered to "Stearnes's Confederate cavalry."

For the month of June 1862, the organization of troops in the Department of East Tennessee, Maj. Gen. E. Kirby Smith commanding, shows Starnes' 3rd Tennessee Cavalry as one of the unattached units. The July 3rd tabulation has the regiment in Col. Benjamin Allston's First Cavalry Brigade of Brig. Gen. Henry Heth's Second Division. These assignment lists had very limited information about the actual operations and make up of the various and changing commands. For all practical purposes, Starnes' regiment was not truly brigaded until Smith's invasion of Kentucky was underway.

Early in July, 1st Lt. Gustave A. Huwald's newly-formed, six-gun Mountain Howitzer Battery came out from Knoxville and was assigned to the 3rd Tennessee Cavalry. Two of the pieces were rifled and four were smooth bores. Each was pulled by one mule while the ammunition was carried on the back of a second mule. Sgt. Tom Tulloss of Company "F" said these guns could go anywhere a mule could walk.

Starnes' popularity as a Rebel cavalry leader in Tennessee was greatly enhanced in July 1862 by premature Federal reports crediting him as the commander of daring attacks by Confederate cavalry, which were actually carried out by others of more fame than himself. On his first raid, Col. John H. Morgan attacked and captured a cavalry post of four companies at Thomkinsville, Kentucky on July 9th. Col. Nathan B. Forrest, on his first raid, surprised the brigade of Brig. Gen. T. L. Crittenden at the town of Murfreesboro on July 13th, captured the general, the entire command (1040 men), and stores worth almost a million dollars. There were persistent concerns expressed in Yankee correspondence between commands that Forrest, Morgan and Starnes would combine forces and fall unexpectedly on some unfortunate fortification or garrison. Despite the extensive fortifications surrounding the large garrison in the occupied capital of Nashville, Col. John F. Miller (29th Indiana Infantry), commanding there, and the Military Governor were both somewhat anxious about being the object of such an attack.

It was probably almost as well known among the Union posts as it was among the Confederates, that Forrest and Starnes both had the hopes and high aspirations of one day retaking their state capital. The former tailor from Greenville, Tennessee, Governor Andrew Johnson, wired Maj. Gen. Henry Halleck July 13th: "Starnes with his division...attacked Murfreesboro this morning... It is reported that Starnes will reach here tonight or in the morning."

In Knoxville July 23, Starnes finally received his March and April lieutenant colonel's pay of $185/month.

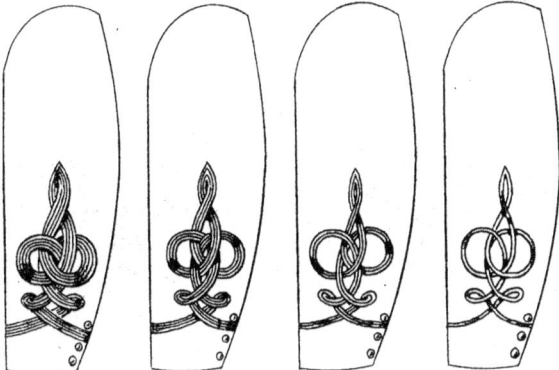

MOUNTAIN ARTILLERY.

SLEEVE BADGES C. S. ARMY

GENERAL   COLONEL   CAPTAIN   LIEUTENANT

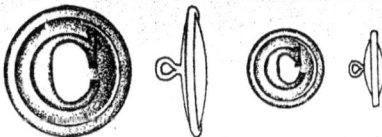

BUTTONS, C. S. ARMY

CAVALRY OFFICERS.

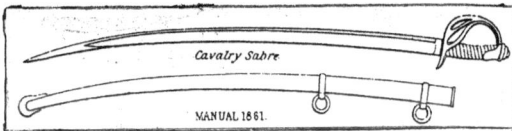

Cavalry Sabre

MANUAL 1861.

THE CONFEDERATE STATES OF AMERICA,

To _J. W. A. Hamer, ..._ Dr.

ON WHAT ACCOUNT.	COMMENCEMENT AND EXPIRATION.		TERM OF SERVICE CHARGED.		PAY PER MONTH.		AMOUNT.		REMARKS.
	From—	To—	Months.	Days.	Dollars.	Cents.	Dollars.	Cents.	
Pay—as a Private									
For myself, ...	March 1st	April 30	2		185		37	10	
For year's service, .									
Forage for horses, .						$	37	10	

I hereby certify that the foregoing account is accurate and just; that I have not been absent, without leave, during any part of the time charged for; that I have not received pay, forage, or received money in lieu of any part thereof, for any part of the time therein charged; that the horses were actually kept in service and were mustered for the whole of the time charged; that for the whole of the time charged for my staff appointment, I actually and legally held the appointment and did duty in the department; that I am not in arrears with the Confederate States on any account whatsoever; and that the last payment I received was from . . . . 18__

I, at the same time, acknowledge that I have received of . . . . and to the . . . . day of . . . . 18__

this _23_ day of _July_ 1862, the sum of . . . . Dollars, being the amount in full of said account.

Pay, - - $ 37.10

Forage, - -

Amount, $37.10

(Signed Duplicates.)

Kirby Smith's Invasion of Kentucky

Generals Bragg and Smith met in Chattanooga in early August and apparently agreed on a general plan for their joint operations in Kentucky. There were two major Union forces they had to consider very seriously. Buell's army was spread out along the railroad southeast of Nashville, all the way into northern Alabama, as he moved ever so slowly on Chattanooga. Brig. Gen. George W. Morgan held Cumberland Gap with 8,000 to 9,000, with the intention of eventually moving south on Knoxville.

On August 4, 1862 Brig. Gen. Forrest, commanding the First Cavalry Brigade, was advised that his orders to move his command to Kingston had been countermanded, that he should stay in Middle Tennessee, and that his Brigadier General's Commission (dated July 21) would be forwarded to him. This correspondence further stated that Col. Starnes' regiment of cavalry and Huwald's howitzer battery had been ordered to join him, but it would probably take them two weeks to reach him.

Gen. Smith ordered Starnes' cavalry and Huwald's battery detached from Brig. Gen. C.L. Stevenson's division and sent to Roger's Gap or Clinton on August 8th. Stevenson must have objected, since on the 9th he advised Stevenson that he "could not spare Starnes' cavalry from the purpose for which he had ordered it detached."

That same date, Smith ordered Col. John S. Scott, commanding the Second Cavalry Brigade at Kingston, to detach Col. John A. Wharton's Texas cavalry regiment from his command and send it to Brig. Gen. N.B. Forrest at Roddy, Tennessee. Scott was promised that Col. J.W. Starnes would join him on the other side of the mountain with his regiment of cavalry.

Bragg's and Smith's armies were still many miles apart as Kirby Smith began moving out of Knoxville at 4 AM on Thursday, August 18, 1862. Bragg was still in Chattanooga trying to get his forces organized and prepared for the long march up to Kentucky. Smith ordered Starnes' Cavalry into Knoxville to lead his column out and over the mountains into Kentucky. But before they could arrive in the city, they were sent to meet the sappers who were on their way to Big Creek Gap to clear the road. The cavalry arrived about the same time as the sappers. The Federals had infantry, cavalry and artillery units out on the road who would certainly have driven off or captured the sappers without a regiment of cavalry there to protect them.

Starnes' troopers were impressed with how rapidly those men cleared the thoroughly blockaded road. Morgan's Union men had cut down all the trees within reach of the road, mostly poplar and oak, in this narrow defile in the Cumberland Mountains, and stacked them to block any passage. As soon as the road was cleared, the march began for the Bluegrass State with Starnes' Cavalry leading the way about 4 PM Saturday, August 16th.

The route taken was well west of the Cumberland Gap, through a remote, sparsely settled area appropriately called "The Barrens." About four miles north of Big Creek Gap, the road forked at the foot of the mountain. The passage across Pine Mountain was rough, rocky and steep. Clear Fork of the Cumberland was forded on its broad, gravelly bottom a little south of the Kentucky state line. In just sixty hours Smith's forces had scrambled over the mountains and were headed into Barboursville, Kentucky.

Col. John Hunt Morgan, a Kentuckian from Lexington, had misled the senior Confederate generals, Bragg and Smith, and indeed, President Jefferson Davis, into believing that Kentuckians would rally to the southern cause en masse. 25,000 recruits for the rebel army were expected. Southern leaders saw themselves as the liberators of a subjugated Kentucky populace.

Alabama Pvt. J.R. Harris, Company "F," and probably his younger brother, Polk Harris, were out front again in the extreme advance of Starnes' cavalry, leading a five-man detail. They were being "bushwhacked" every few hundred yards by citizens, he said. Several were captured. Harris got one out of a hollow log. At that time the military justice systems of both armies provided for the prompt execution of a civilian caught participating in military combat. The wife of the man came screaming out of a nearby cabin begging for his life, followed by some ten to a dozen children. The matter was referred to Gen. Smith, who turned the man over to his better half. Harris and his detail made the poor fellow and his wife kiss the Bible and swear they would be non-combatants in the forever future before letting him go, Sunday, August 17th.

A little further up the road they captured a lieutenant and fourteen men in a scouting detail, who were the first Yankee soldiers they had encountered on the march. The next morning they dashed into Barboursville, capturing "a lot of mules, wagons and soldiers with government supplies."

Just out of Barboursville at a spring, Harris and Pvt. Tom Hunt, Company "C," came upon four surgeons in the company of four young ladies and demanded surrender. One of the doctors requested that Harris bring his colonel forward to accept the surrender since that was the doctor's rank. Harris squinted down his buckshot-loaded, double-barreled shotgun and replied, "No foolishness." The surrender was promptly offered.

Hunt and Harris thought all those young ladies were pretty, but one of them verbally abused these two dirty, ragged cavalrymen very much, saying that if she had a gun she would shoot Harris. "Ole J.R.," who claimed the first shot of the war fired on Alabama soil was fired at him, offered her a pistol. He said that he believed she would have shot him if she had gotten it from his grasp. She would not have missed, as had a landing party crew member from the blockading vessel at Navy Cove near Fort Morgan, Alabama.

Starnes' original company, the sons of his county's most prominent families, was, by this time (due to casualties, transfers, desertions, recruitment, etc.), made up of two-thirds Alabamians and one-third Tennesseans. Harris was one of those Cotton State recruits.

Barboursville was a hotbed of Unionists. Scant food and forage, bad water and pro-Union bushwhackers everywhere, made Smith's occupation an unpleasant situation. From this place he had gotten behind George Morgan's 8,000 Federals in the Cumberland Gap, but decided the place was too strong to attack, even from the rear. Smith divided his forces on the march from Knoxville, sending Stevenson with 9,000 men to keep pressure on Morgan from the Tennessee front of the Gap's fortifications.

Col. J.S. Scott left Kingston on the 13th of August, attacked and captured London, Kentucky on the 17th, and promptly requested that Starnes be sent to him. On the 23rd he moved toward Richmond, defeating two Federal regiments at Big Hill, the 7th Kentucky Cavalry and a battalion of the 3rd Tennessee Infantry. Scott had intended to occupy Crab Orchard, but a brigade of Union cavalry under Brig. Gen. G.L. Smith had already arrived there. He had hoped to have been reinforced by Starnes' regiment by this time, but planned to take Richmond without it. From documents found in the captured coat of the Union colonel commanding at Big Hill, Scott learned that reinforcements of a brigade of infantry and four pieces of artillery were on their way from Lexington. He fell back to Big Hill on the 24th.

On that date, Kirby Smith, despite Bragg's advice against it, left Barboursville and started north again toward the bluegrass country. Starnes joined Scott on the 27th with Huwald's Battery of six mountain howitzers. Scott had four smooth-bore, brass cannon.

Early the next morning cavalry scouting parties were sent in the direction of Richmond. About 10 AM, dispatches were sent back reporting a large cavalry force advancing from that town. Scott's and Starnes' men dismounted and the horses were sent back out of sight. The batteries were placed in position and the troopers deployed for an ambush. There was a long wait, but the gunfire could be heard as the scouting parties fell back. Their orders were to retreat up the hill where their comrades were under cover and draw them into their line of fire. One of the waiting troopers said that when they came in sight, the scouts "were putting in their best licks running and never even slowed down for the hill, but came on as fast as they could."

The Federal cavalry was allowed to get near the top of the hill before a gun was fired. Then the small arms and artillery opened together on them. The effect on the men and horses was devastating. Starnes and Scott followed the escaping cavalry to a position near Richmond where a large force of Federal infantry was encamped. They then returned to camp near Big Hill for the night.

On the 29th, the whole cavalry brigade made a reconnaissance of the enemy's position and found them three miles from Richmond with a very large infantry force. Scott and Starnes did not elect to attack, and slowly fell back toward Big Hill. That afternoon they ran into a contingent of Yankee cavalry near the village of Rogersville, seven miles south of Richmond.

Those blue-clad horsemen went dashing back to their commanding general's headquarters, saying they were being pressed hard by 4,000 to 5,000 Rebels. Scott's brigade had about 900 men on the reconnaissance, including the artillery. Brig. Gen. Mahlon Manson did not know where his senior officer was. Maj. Gen. Don Carlos Buell, commanding the Union Department of the Ohio, had sent his best division leader, Maj. Gen. William "Bull" Nelson, up from Tennessee to command the green troops being assembled in Kentucky to oppose Kirby Smith's advance. Manson did know that the enemy was advancing on him in considerable force; so he ordered his two small divisions to head south toward the Rebel army encampments.

The Rebel cavalry brigade's rear guard had drifted off beside the Lexington road into the cover of the woods, from where they watched the Union advance. A battery fired on them and drove them from cover. Skirmishers from the 55th Indiana Infantry pursued them so rapidly that one of Starnes' mountain howitzers was captured just before 5 PM. A short time later, Scott and Starnes rode in with the main body of the brigade. Starnes' men went into camp on one side of the road and Scott's on the other.

Col. Scott went to report to Brig. Gen. Patrick Cleburne (from Bragg's army), commanding the leading division of Kirby Smith's forces. Cleburne had heard the artillery firing up the road and was concerned about what it meant. Scott assured him that the enemy was not moving forward and that their front was well picketed. The Irishman was not so sure about that. He had earlier placed a company of sharpshooters in advance of his main lines. Cleburne had his regimental commanders form their men in line of battle, and instructed them to take those positions if there was an alarm. Just after the regimental officers shouted, "Dismissed," a motley band of Scott's and Starnes' stragglers rode into camp with the devil himself, in the form of Union cavalry, right behind them, armed with breech-loading, Sharps carbines. And they were shouting, "Charge and shoot down the Rebels!"

Cleburne's marksmen held their fire until their cavalry had passed, then opened up from a range of about 25 paces. Bravely, the Yankees dismounted in the deepening dusk and fired wildly at distant campfires. A volley from a company of the 48th Tennessee sent them cursing and swearing revenge in the direction from whence they had come. Two dead, two wounded, thirty prisoners, and 100 Sharps carbines that could fire three times faster than any muzzle loader, were left behind. Cleburne's men were very unhappy with the cavalry for having caused the scuffle that deprived them of their dinner, even if it was mostly roasted ears of green corn.

That night Col. Starnes went to see Gen. Smith, who had decided to attack at Big Hill, rather than delay and have a difficult and bloody fight along the bluffs of the Kentucky River. His troopers figured the subject of the colonel's meeting with the general was plans for battle. Starnes had a large, bay mare that he never rode except when he expected a battle. Early the next morning his men's anticipation was confirmed, their colonel was mounted on that mare. The colonel, on the right of the Confederate force, moved his regiment out and placed it around Richmond on the east side, and three pieces of Huwald's Battery were positioned to command the Lexington Pike for a distance of about half a mile. This position, and those taken by Scott's cavalry, was to the rear of the Federals and without infantry support.

During the night Smith had sent word to Cleburne that he should attack in the morning. Scott's Buckner Guards, a company of horsemen under Capt. Garnett, spread out in the lead of the infantry advance from Big Hill. About a half-mile north of the village of Kingston, the cavalry made contact with Manson's lines on both sides of the Richmond Road. Cleburne formed his battle lines, then came under what he called, "a ridiculous fire," from the mountain howitzer that Starnes and Huwald had lost to capture the afternoon before. The annoyed Irishman brought up his own battery and sent snipers to pick off the enemy gunners and artillery horses. Kirby Smith sent up orders to delay a full attack until Brig. Gen. Thomas J. Churchill's division arrived from Big Hill. Cleburne had his batteries fire at a slow rate, as the artillery dueled for about two hours.

Manson brought up Brig. Gen. Charles Cruft's brigade from Richmond and placed it on the left side of his line near Mt. Zion Church. Cruft's men surged forward and the battle was on. Cleburne rushed reinforcements to meet Cruft's advance, and correctly anticipated Churchill's arrival and advance on the Confederate left. There were about forty minutes of continuous firing between the Confederate veterans and the Union recruits. By 3 PM, the men on both sides had been in action almost eight hours under a blistering sun and with little water to drink. The Federal lines gave way, and men in blue were running in droves from all directions through the cornfields for Richmond.

Kirby Smith had arrived on the field of battle delighted at the retreat of Manson's raw recruits. Manson was a former druggist and Indiana state legislator. He had been a general for three months, Cruft for six weeks. Both were political appointees by the governor of the Hoosier State. They had scarcely more military experience than the green troops they commanded. Actually, the Federal recruits fought as well as could have been expected against veteran Confederates.

Smith was puzzled by the loud cheer that went up from the rear of the retreating Yankees. The cheer was for the arrival of General "Bull" Nelson who had been riding since 2:30 AM for over 50 miles, from Lexington by the back roads, to avoid Scott's and Starnes' cavalry north of Richmond.

The six-foot-five, over 300-pound Nelson by his sheer size and brute personality, was able to rally some 2,500 panic-stricken recruits on a hill near Richmond. He cursed the Indianians as cowardly poor trash who descended from Rebel hillbillies, while whacking some of those who were least inclined to fight with the flat of his sword. And, by God, he was going to straighten them out.

Nelson deployed the troops in the town's cemetery behind a stone wall. Smith's men formed a mile away, and were so tired they just walked slowly up the hill to the attack. Nelson dismounted and paced back and forth behind his lines, bellowing like the male bovine his sobriquet suggested. To those concerned about being targets for the rebel sharpshooters, he roared out, "If they can't hit me they can't hit anything." Almost immediately, two bullets hit his thigh. One Rebel division began enveloping Nelson's right flank, the other his left. After three volleys, Nelson's troops at the cemetery fence were running through Richmond, trying to overtake the others who had run through the town ahead of them. Much to their displeasure, an unexpected Rebel maneuver awaited.

The running recruits in blue ran right into the leveled shotguns and few rifles of "The Kirby Smith Brigade," as Scott chose to call his small cavalry command of the 1st Georgia, 1st Louisiana and 3rd Tennessee.

Col. Starnes had stationed his old company "F" on the Lexington Pike. Capt. McLemore and his men were understandably nervous in this primary position on the main thoroughfare to Lexington, with a major battle going on to the south of them. McLemore had only about thirty men that morning. All morning they had heard artillery and rifle fire, which increased in intensity in the afternoon. And they had not had a single word about what was going on only three miles south of their position.

Before noon, straggling parties of Federals began to come along up the road. There was a lot nearby that was enclosed by a high, plank fence. The Rebel cavalrymen opened the gate and ordered the retreating parties of Manson's and Cruft's recruits to "Throw down your guns and go into the lot." They were so demoralized and depressed by their misfortunes at the front that they obeyed without question, and made no attempt to escape. The flow of retreating Yankees on the road increased in the afternoon to a tide.

A quick-acting, Yankee cavalry major helped the wounded Bull Nelson up onto his horse and led him up a side road past Starnes' and Scott's cavalry, who were so busy taking captives and watching others disappear through the cornfields that they were not alert to the possibility of capturing the rather elephantine commanding general. But Pvt. Joe Balanfont, of Company "F," from the whistle-stop of Culleoka on the Tennessee & Alabama RR south of Columbia, Tennessee, captured the second in command, Mahlon Manson.

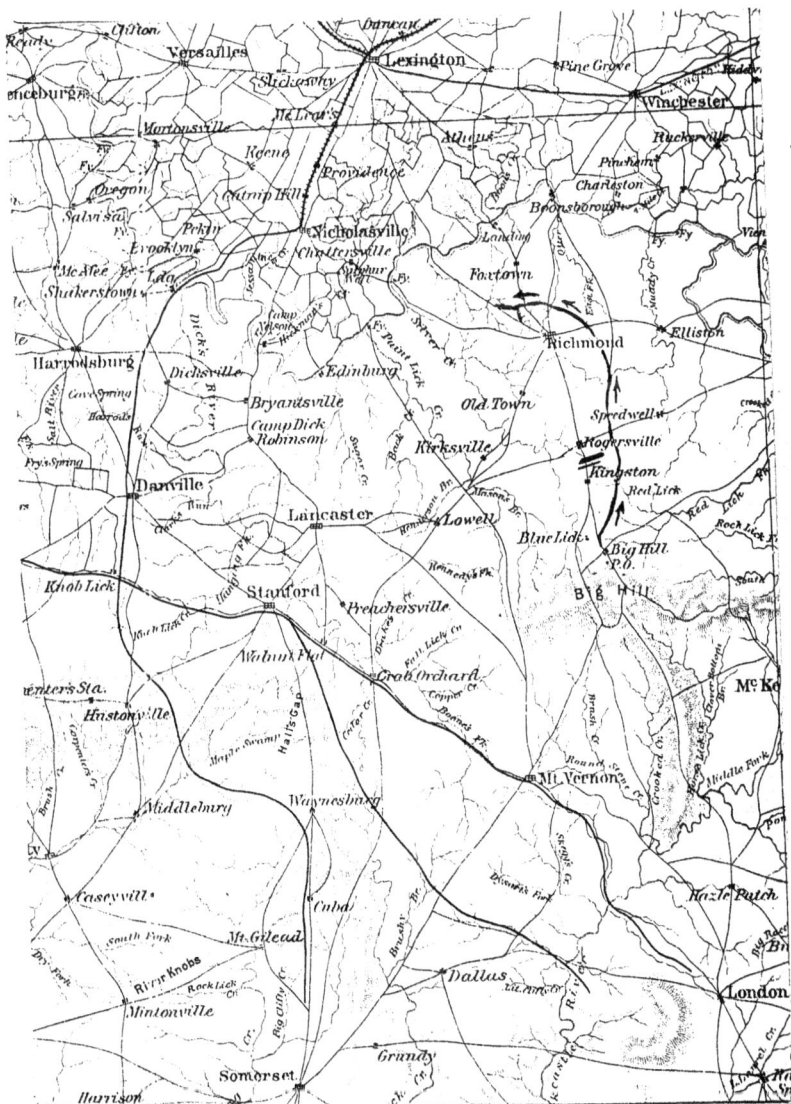

Movement of Starnes' Cavalry (indicated by arrows) **the early morning of August 30, 1862 to the position taken on the Lexington Pike where the large number of prisoners were captured that afternoon**

Battle Site about a mile north of the village of Kingston

Union line ⬛
Confederate line ⟋

Brig. Gen. Manson had lost his horse and was trying to escape on foot. Balanfont came riding in with the slightly wounded Manson in front of him on his horse, and marching ten privates ahead of the horse into the lot for the captives.

When the wagons and artillery began heading towards Lexington, Capt. Huwald blocked the road with broken wagons and dead horses by a few well-directed shots from the mountain howitzers. All the wagons and artillery to the rear had been captured by the Rebels.

In the late afternoon, Capt. McLemore sent two of his men towards Richmond to find out how the battle had gone, with orders " to return as soon as possible." They forgot to return. McLemore was beside himself with many more prisoners than it was possible to guard, and still no word on the battle. He kept his men and himself busy all night, stopping men and wagons and standing guard. It wasn't until early next morning, September 1st, that they heard that Kirby Smith had won "a great victory." The wagons were hitched up and driven toward Richmond.

With a few of his men and Gen. Manson by his side, Capt. McLemore rode in front of the wagons. The prisoners marched in file behind the wagons with the rest of the company in the rear. Col. Starnes credited Company "F" with the capture of 1,000 men.

In Lexington that night, Bull Nelson counted up his losses while first a rifle ball was removed from his leg and the other "through bullet hole" attended and dressed; 206 killed, 844 wounded, 4,303 captured or missing. Kirby Smith's losses were 78 killed, 372 wounded and one missing.

Scott's cavalry moved up and camped near Lexington on September 1st as Nelson and his defeated recruits, who could hardly be called an army, retreated toward Louisville.

On the 2nd, Scott and Starnes moved around Lexington and went into camp at the settlement of Georgetown, north of the city. Kirby Smith entered Lexington with his occupying force to the display of Confederate flags, girls and women waving from every window, baskets of food and flowers and buckets of cool water for the tired, dirty, ragged Confederates. The next day tho place went absolutely wild with jubilation when the local hero, Col. John Hunt Morgan, and his men rode in at the gallop.

Starnes, Scott and the "Kirby Smith Brigade" didn't take part in the huge victory celebration. They were ordered to seize the state capitol. On the 3rd they rode into Frankfort and hoisted the colors of the 1st Louisiana Cavalry over the capitol building, since there was not a Confederate flag to be found among them. The rear guard of Nelson's 8,000-man retreating Union force "were quiet spectators from the opposite hills."

That same evening, Col. Scott detailed all of his command with horses in condition to travel, some 450 in number, to pursue the enemy and harass their rear. About sunrise the next morning, September 4th, they came upon the enemy near Shelbyville. Col. Starnes, with the mountain howitzer battery and 600 cavalry, attacked a strong enemy column of 9,000 men and nine pieces of artillery. This bold attack drove the Federals, who must have assumed the cavalry and howitzers were the advance of Kirby Smith's army, through the town and out toward Louisville, 28 miles away. The cavalry then crossed over the railroad spur from the Louisville, Frankfort & Lexington RR and destroyed the bridges in accordance with Kirby Smith's orders. They advanced to within 12 miles of Louisville, then returned to camp near Frankfort where they remained through the 7th of September. On the evening of the 8th, the cavalry left Frankfort and arrived in Lebanon at 9 AM on the 11th. The evening before, Starnes had reported from Taylorsville.

Scott and Starnes were ordered to join Gen. Bragg's advance forces at Munfordville on the Green River, about 45 miles north of the Tennessee state line. They arrived on September 13th. This town's main fortification was a heavy stockade with four cannon west of the Louisville & Nashville RR. Scott sent in a surrender demand about 8 PM. Col. John T. Wilder, commanding the garrison of three Indiana regiments, refused.

Brig. Gen. James R. Chalmers' Mississippi brigade arrived during the night, and at 5 AM, supported by Huwald's Battery, assaulted the stockade and blockhouse on the opposite side of the railroad track.

Starnes had positioned his regiment just across the river from the fort on a high bluff. From that vantage point, they witnessed Chalmers' attack with five regiments of infantry. One of Starnes' men said, "It was a fool thing to do, but it looked for awhile like they were going to take the fort, but failed with heavy loss."

When Chalmers withdrew from the attack, the Federals fired one shot at Starnes' men across the river, killing one man. That young man was Pvt. John Cartright, who had close relatives back in Franklin, Tennessee. He lived nearby and had enlisted only a few hours earlier in Company "F" when the regiment had arrived in town.

About 9:30 AM Chalmers again demanded surrender, and again Wilder refused. Late that night of the 14th, reinforcements of seven companies sneaked past Scott's pickets and into the fort, though he did capture some of them. A stagnant siege existed on the 14th and 15th. Bragg's forces arrived on the 15th and he prepared to make a major assault. Wilder, an Indiana industrialist without military experience, asked to see Confederate Maj. Gen. Simon B. Buckner for advice. Buckner politely received him, discussed military position, command responsibility and options, but offered no advice.

Buckner took Wilder to see Bragg and then gave him a tour of the forces arrayed against him, pointing out the extent of the besieging lines and artillery emplacements. Col. Wilder chose to surrender in a formal ceremony on the morning of the 17th. Brig. Gen. George Washington Morgan was at that time evacuating his Federal troops from Cumberland Gap.

Gen. Chalmers, having carefully studied the battleground following the surrender, believed his initial attack would have succeeded, had not Huwald's Battery opened unexpectedly from a hill to his rear, to support his Mississippi boys. The Mississippians thought that somehow the Yankees had positioned a battery behind them. Chalmers ordered the 7th and 9th Mississippi regiments to face about and charge the battery. With two regiments coming at them, Huwald's five mountain howitzers began a hurried withdrawal before being recognized as attached to Col. Scott's cavalry.

This place, astride a vital supply route, would have been a good location in which to force a major battle. Bragg remained there until the 20th waiting for Buell to attack him, then moved north to Bardstown. Buell's forces reached Munfordville the following day.

Kirby Smith had about 21,000 men, but he spread his forces a bit too thin and split his army: 3,000 were chasing and trying to cut off George Morgan' retreat from the Cumberland Gap at Covington, Kentucky on the Ohio River; there were about 8,000 rebels left to garrison the gap, and the rest had a large area of eastern Kentucky to hold. By the 19th of September, Smith was concerned about the lack of cavalry coverage to his rear, and sent a dispatch to Bragg complaining that his orders to Col. Scott to return to Richmond had been countermanded. Smith and Bragg had outmaneuvered and outmarched their opponents, but time was turning against them as Buell's larger forces were slowly closing in.

Col. Starnes' regiment was to operate "in front of Frankfort toward Louisville," and the rest of Scott's brigade was to go to Irvine via Richmond. Bragg persisted in keeping them all in the capital area.

Bragg disposed his army in the vicinity of Bardstown on September 23rd. Buell's leading troops reached Louisville on the 29th, where Bull Nelson had 39,700 raw recruits under his command. But Maj. Gen. William "Bull" Nelson was dead.

That Monday morning Brig. Gen. Jefferson C. Davis entered Nelson's headquarters in the Galt House Hotel. Davis had incurred Nelson's criticism, due to his handling of the local home guards. The two exchanged words and Nelson slapped Davis in the face, calling him a "Damned Puppy." Davis stepped into the lobby and borrowed a pistol. He then shot Nelson as he was ascending the stairs, favoring his wounded leg from the Battle of Richmond, Kentucky two months before.

Gen. Forrest had caught up with Bragg's army at Glasgow, Kentucky on September 10th, and participated in the capture of Munfordville by blocking the Federal escape route north along the railroad. His brigade was temporarily attached to Maj. Gen. Leonidas Polk's division where he operated along the Louisville & Nashville RR in the Bardstown area. Forrest received a letter asking him to report in person to Gen. Bragg's headquarters. There, on the last day of the month, he was directed to turn over command of the brigade he had personally organized in Chattanooga to Col. John A. Wharton of the Texas Rangers. Forrest was allowed to keep his staff and four companies of Alabamians as escorts, and was ordered to establish headquarters at Murfreesboro and to recruit and organize a new brigade of six regiments.

Buell integrated Nelson's raw troops into his veteran divisions and began to move out of Louisville on October 1st to do battle with Bragg.

Col. Scott advised Col. Wharton on the 3rd that the enemy was advancing on the Louisville and Shelbyville road. That Friday evening and the morning of Saturday, the 4th, the Confederates massed troops at Frankfort, as well as a number of high ranking officers, including Bragg and Smith. At 11 AM, after the ceremonies of inaugurating a Confederate governor of Kentucky had begun, the Kirby Smith Brigade had a skirmish three miles out of Clay Village with the advance guards of Col. Edward N. Kirk's 5th Brigade, and suffered some casualties and captures. At noon Richard Hawes, a former C.S.A. brigade commissary Major and Provisional Governor, was sworn in as governor of the Bluegrass State. By 3 PM the rebels began to evacuate the city, burned the railroad bridge and destroyed the flooring and timbers of the Louisville turnpike bridge over the Kentucky River.

At sunrise on October 5th, Scott was at Frankfort and Starnes' regiment was on the west side of the Kentucky River. Since their return from Munfordville, they had been operating much as separate commands.

On the 6th, Col. Scott was ordered to report through Brig. Gen. C.L. Stevenson, commanding at Versailles, Kentucky. If Scott did not obey orders from Stevenson, Smith directed Stevenson to arrest the commanding officer of the Kirby Smith Cavalry Brigade.

The next day Scott reported that an enemy force, that he estimated at 20,000, had crossed the Kentucky River at Frankfort and drove in his pickets at the Georgetown and Frankfort road. These forces were the divisions of Brig. Gens. Joshua W. Sill and Ebenezer Dumont that Scott had previously reported moving from Louisville in that direction .

Gen. Sill moved away on the 8th at 1 PM toward Lawrenceberg. Part of Dumont's heavy division of four infantry brigades, three light batteries and five companies of cavalry attacked the Confederates in the city. The Rebels were driven out of town down the Versailles road to their encampment.

Dumont brought his main force across the river for the fight and pursuit, but he found the road "unavailing to station my artillery." The whole engagement lasted about six hours. Starnes and Scott reconsolidated to do what they could to harass the attackers and cover the Confederate retreat during the continuing worst drought in years and an unusually warm autumn. By the waning light of day, with every Union cavalry unit in the area forming to catch them, Starnes and Scott made for the safety of the Confederate divisions. At about dark they reached the heavy stone bridge across the Kentucky River at Frankfort with Yankee cavalry in close pursuit.

A small rear guard was left at the bridge. From the bridge the road led up a steep hill with a stone fence on the left. The rest of the command dismounted and took position behind the stone fence, while the horse holders led their mounts over the crest of the hill. The rear guard held the bridge as long as possible, then came up the hill "at a safe gait, closely followed by the enemy." Fire was held until the bridge defenders reached the top of the hill, then shotguns loaded with buckshot blazed away from the stone wall into the pursuing cavalrymen. The survivors quickly recrossed the river and made no further advance. When the dismounted men came over the hill to remount, the others asked, "Did you hurt anybody?"

"Yes," they said, "we killed them all."

Meanwhile, near Perryville in the morning, several ill-directed divisions from both Buell's and Bragg's armies had collided in a vicious battle. Some of the fighting was for possession of a supply of drinking water from the few pools in the drought-stricken countryside. The engagement ended at dark with heavy casualties on both sides. Federal losses were 845 killed, 2,850 wounded, and 515 missing from a force of 37,000 (not all were committed to battle). Of 16,000 Confederate effectives, 510 were killed, 2,635 wounded, and 250 missing. Nothing of any consequence was accomplished for either side in taking those heavy casualties, which included two Union generals killed and three Confederate generals wounded.

With an outnumbering force, Buell determined to renew the battle on the morning of the 9th, but Bragg withdrew during the night to Harrodsburg toward Kirby Smith. The southern high water mark had been reached in the west. There was no rising of Kentuckians to join the Rebel cause. Before Perryville, Confederate casualties were greater in number than those recruited. Smith and Bragg were never able to coordinate their efforts, and appeared to have no definite objectives once they were deep into Kentucky. Smith had accomplished some small, initial success, Bragg nothing.

Pursuit of the Confederates began on the 10th. Their forces withdrew from Harrodsburg, which was reoccupied by the Federals on the 11th. Scott and Starnes had arrived and taken position near Camp Dick Robinson, in the Bryantsville area, to cover the troops massing for a retreat to Tennessee.

A dispatch to Col. Scott on October 12th said Smith hoped the colonel could hold his position. If not, he should fall back slowly toward Nicholasville. At 3 AM the following morning, by Special Order No. 14, Col. Joseph Wheeler was appointed Chief of Cavalry, reporting to Kirby Smith, with all cavalry reporting to Wheeler and receiving his orders.

The army was to move by one route to Lancaster where it would divide into two columns, one moving by way of Crab Orchard, the other by Big Hill. At Lancaster the cavalry would be divided, with half following the Army of the Mississippi and the other half following the Army of Kentucky to Big Hill.

Scott and Starnes, like many others, were near disgust with their higher ranked commanders. Now they were to take orders from a 25-year-old West Pointer as Chief of Cavalry, who wore a beard to conceal his youthful appearance.

At Camp Dick Robinson, Starnes had had his courier, young Sam Claybrooke, sent to him, and he asked the 16-year-old lad if he thought he could ride alone through the mountains and deliver a letter to Gen. Forrest in Murfreesboro.

Samuel P., the youngest son of Col. John S. Claybrooke, had left school in Murfreesboro and joined Starnes' cavalry company shortly before he was 15 years old. At the request of his father, Governor Isham Harris ordered Starnes to discharge him as underage for service. "S.P." went home to Triune, Tennessee for awhile, but after the occupation of Nashville he made his way between the lines back to Starnes at Jasper, Tennessee. Starnes refused to allow him to be sworn in, but did agree to have him serve as a soldier and do as he pleased. Claybrooke, whose older brother was a major in the 20th Tennessee Infantry, voluntarily did picket duty, camp duty and everything else expected of a soldier. He drew rations for himself and a servant, refused pay, and bought his own boots and clothes. Claybrooke's first engagement was at Readyville, and he had fought or held horses in every encounter since then.

The boy assured the colonel he could safely get through to Gen. Forrest. Starnes then wrote a personal dispatch asking Forrest to order the regiment to his command in Murfreesboro.

On the 13th Col. Scott's command was ordered to move in the direction of Col. Wheeler, en route to Crab Orchard. Col. John A. Wharton, the Texan now in command of Forrest's old brigade, was hard pressed and looking for Scott to help him cover the rear or protect the right flank of the column passing by way of Crab Orchard. A heavy force of infantry, supported by artillery with cavalry, drove Wharton's horse soldiers out of Stanford. He then moved down the road near Crab Orchard.

On the morning of October 14th Col. Scott wrote a dispatch explaining the situation of his command:

Colonel Wheeler:

My command is 2 miles from Crab Orchard, on the road leading to Stanford. My Brigade is about 1,000 strong. My horses are very much jaded, having been in front of Maj. Gen. E. Kirby Smith's army since his entrance into Kentucky. I consulted General Bragg this morning, and he consented that I should take my command via Somerset, in order that I might procure forage on that route, unless my services are absolutely required to assist you in getting out, in which case I am at your service. I shall, however, remain in my present position until I hear from you.

Very respectfully,

J.S. Scott
Colonel Commanding Brigade

In the afternoon, some hours after the army had passed, Col. Wharton arrived near Crab Orchard and sent a 4 PM dispatch to Col. Wheeler and repeated his 2 PM message: "Scott has gone to Somerset."

Kirby Smith was very concerned that the Crab Orchard defile be kept occupied by the cavalry, since it gave the enemy "a passage to my flank." Burdened with his baggage and supply train and many of Gen. Bragg's wagons, Smith's forces moved slowly on the rough roads.

An October 15th, 6:30 AM dispatch from Maj. George Wm. Brent, Smith's Chief of Staff and Asst. Adjutant-General, was a message from the road three miles out of Mount Vernon toward London, Kentucky to Col. Wheeler at Crab Orchard, Kentucky saying that Col. Scott had been arrested for disobedience of orders and his command turned over to the next in rank (Starnes). And he was ordered to report to Col. Wharton for duty. During the night Wharton had been ordered to "send in pursuit" of Scott's command and turn it back to the aid of Col. Wheeler.

About eight miles south of Somerset at the crossing of the Cumberland River, the enemy attacked and routed Colonels Scott's and Starnes' cavalry. Col. James R. Howard's 3rd Confederate Cavalry pickets heard the firing, and Howard took his command to the rear to assist them.

But by the time he arrived they had left with the enemy in full pursuit. Union cavalry followed Scott and Starnes south to the area of Monticello and then turned back. "They followed us no further, we were on our way into Tennessee and were not molested," said trooper Tom Tulloss.

Starnes and Scott parted company when they got into Tennessee. Starnes moved as quickly as his worn out horses and men could travel to join Gen. Forrest in Murfreesboro. Starnes' men had been impressed with Col. Scott during their service in his small cavalry brigade in Kentucky, but never knew what became of him: "He was as gallant a soldier as ever rode a horse."

Apparently nothing became of the attempt to arrest Col. Scott, since he had the permission of the senior commanding general to move his brigade via Somerset, covering part of Bragg's Army's retreat. This assignment was preferable to that of reporting to and receiving orders from the youthful Col. Joseph Wheeler. Col. Starnes was also anxious to take this shorter route back to Middle Tennessee and report to Gen. Forrest.

Pvt. W.H. Whittsitt, who had "found an empty saddle" in Starnes' Battalion at Winchester, Tennessee the last of April when they had come over from Chattanooga on a scouting expedition, remarked:

> It was a special mercy for us that General Buell was not more vigorous and successful in the military art. If he had been a genuine soldier, we might have had some trouble getting out of Kentucky; but after delivering battle at Perryville we got off very light and made our escape.

Starnes' Cavalry Route During Smith's and Bragg's Invasion of Kentucky Aug.–Sept. 1862
Knoxville to La Vergne

Forrest's New Brigade

After having been relieved of his command in Kentucky on September 30, 1862, Forrest was back in Tennessee within the first week of October setting up a recruitment bureau in Murfreesboro. Col. Starnes' former Lieutenant Colonel of the 1st Tennessee Volunteer Infantry during the Mexican War, Samuel R. Anderson, had assembled a Confederate force of about 1,700 untried militia (during Buell's pullout of forces to follow Bragg into Kentucky). Rumors spread in the capital that a Confederate attempt to retake the city was imminent. Thinking that there were few Federal combat troops still in the city, Anderson sent a formal demand of surrender to Gen. Negley, the post commander. Negley certainly had enough troops to handle any attack that could be mounted by a force the size of Anderson's, and refused the request on September 29th.

Anderson lived in Nashville and had been postmaster and president of the Bank of Tennessee before he resigned to become Major General, Provisional Army of Tennessee in May, and Brigadier General, C.S.A. in July 1861. He had resigned his C.S.A. commission on May 10, 1862.

With his inexperienced militia and some of Forrest's raw cavalry recruits, Anderson did not want to do battle in the city streets. He waited in La Vergne until Federal troops came out after him on October 7th. Meanwhile, threats to the security of the Tennessee capital were so numerous that the Nashville *Daily Union* couldn't print them all.

Brig. Gen. John M. Palmer's force of 400 cavalry and 4000 infantry came down the Nashville to Murfreesboro road. A force of 1,800 infantry, under Col. John F. Miller, approached by a circuitous route. Anderson was led to believe the entire attacking force was on the road, and opened the first shot with his three pieces of artillery at a range of 300 yards. A responding shot hit the Confederate ammunition chest, silencing Anderson's guns. As the untried Rebels directed their movements on Palmer's right, Col. Miller's infantry arrived and delivered a fire into their ranks. The new Confederate troops held their ground for 30 minutes, when the engagement quickly turned into a rout. Anderson escaped capture by telling the troops he was "going for reinforcements" and fleeing soon after the action had begun. Shortly thereafter the general resigned his provisional army commission.

Col. Starnes joined Gen. Forrest at Murfreesboro about the 18th of October. One of the troopers said that they found Gen. Forrest with a "hand full of raw troops with which he was trying to take Nashville."

Huwald's Battery of mountain howitzers did not report to Gen. Forrest along with Starnes as originally ordered. It arrived in Sparta on the 22nd, was sent to Knoxville, and arrived on the 26th to be refitted. There the battery remained for about three months, recruiting and refitting.

At Murfreesboro Forrest organized and recruited his most famous cavalry brigade consisting of Starnes' 4th, Col. George G. Dibrell's 8th, and Col. Jacob B. Biffle's 9th Tennessee regiments, along with Col. A.A. Russell's 4th Alabama regiment, and one battery of artillery under Capt. Samuel L. Freeman and Lieutenant John W. Morton. Starnes' 4th Tennessee had seen much service, as had the four companies of Col. Russell's regiment that were with Forrest's first battalion at Sacramento in December of 1861. All the others were newly enlisted, although a few may have had some previous service in other military organizations.

Sgt. T.R. Tulloss said that the men in Starnes' regiment were the best armed and had muzzle-loading shot guns. Dibrell's regiment was armed with over 400 old, flintlock rifles of the War of 1812 vintage. Most all the others were armed with flintlock muskets, shotguns, fowling pieces and squirrel rifles brought from home or donated by the Confederate citizenry.

Bragg had promised Forrest command in Middle Tennessee when he had relieved him of brigade command in Kentucky during the last week of September. Large reinforcements were on their way to Forrest, according to an October 21st dispatch from the Knoxville Headquarters of the Department of East Tennessee. On October 27th Maj. Gen. John C. Breckinridge arrived at Murfreesboro with the infantry brigade of Col. Roger W. Hanson, and orders to assume command from Forrest.

Gen. Forrest dutifully moved his command to La Vergne, near Nashville. He and others continued to harass any Union pickets or details that ventured out of the fortifications which were under construction around the city. He was also busy talking Breckinridge into an attack on the capital.

About the first day of November Col. Starnes sent Pvt. Whittsitt, who was a local boy, to report to cavalry headquarters to serve as a guide. "W.H." had never met Gen. Forrest and was nervous about guiding a large body of troops for the first time. But he rode with Forrest all day between the Nolensville and Granny White Pikes while they skirmished with the large detail Gen. Negley had sent out of Nashville on the Franklin Pike, who were to go as far as Brentwood to procure provisions. Provisions were in short supply in the capital, with a 10,000-man garrison and Confederate cavalry, partisan rangers and bushwhackers constantly firing on any Federals they saw.

That night they camped at Nolensville, twelve miles from their encampment at La Vergne. For almost a week Starnes' men were in the saddle about every day " entertaining the garrison at Nashville and trying to worry them into submission before relief {Gen. Buell's returning army under command of Maj. Gen. William S. Rosecrans as of October 30th} might appear." On November 2nd the Wilson County recruits arrived at La Vergne. This resulted in a roster of about 180 men and boys in Company "C."

The new men were furnished with any and all available arms: captured Enfield rifles, Belgian muskets, shotguns, and what were called "Mississippi Rifles." These latter weapons were not the U.S. Rifle Model 1841, made after 1847, which were called Mississippi Rifles in the prewar U.S. Army. The term the Rebel cavalry used probably referred to "homemade" and nondescript pieces made in small shops in several towns and cities, often behind enemy lines, and smuggled south.

On the night of November 4th the cavalry moved forward on seven turnpikes to the city from the east and the south. About daylight of the 5th, with the 4th Alabama Cavalry leading the main column of the infantry brigades of Colonels J.B. Palmer and R.W. Hanson, and four batteries commanded by Maj. R.E. Graves, the Rebels drove in the pickets on the Murfreesboro Pike. When the advance reached Dog Town, the cavalry dismounted and drove the Federal pickets into the fortifications. Having gained the position of a log fortification on a hill near the pike, Forrest opened with a rifle battery of four guns on Jones' Hill, 1 and 1/2 miles away.

Firing was heard from Edgefield on the north side of the Cumberland River, as Brig. Gen. John H. Morgan's cavalry from Gallatin attacked the rail yard. About this time Col. Starnes opened fire on the Nolensville Pike. Gen. Forrest had ordered him, along with Dibrell's regiment and Maj. D.C. Douglass' battalion, and Captains S. L. Freeman's and Frank Roberts' batteries, to move down the Nolensville, Mill Creek and Franklin Pikes.

The engagement then became general, in Forrest's words. Freeman's and Roberts' batteries opened on St. Cloud's Hill where the construction of Fort Negley was nearing completion. For about two hours, until 10 AM, an artillery duel ensued. Breckinridge ordered the infantry to return to camp.

Gen. Forrest ordered Starnes' and Dibrell's regiments and the two batteries to a position five miles out on the Franklin Pike. Gen. Negley had set an ambush for them of four infantry regiments, 12 pieces of artillery and a cavalry battalion. Forrest rode up to place the batteries and return Negley's fire. His guide, Pvt. W.H. Whittsitt from Starnes' company "F," recognized the six-foot battery commander of six brass howitzers, Capt. Freeman, as his former headmaster at the nearby Mill Creek Academy on his mother's farm.

To get to the Franklin Pike, Col. Starnes led his regiment west, to their left, and under a bridge over a dry branch on the Tennessee & Alabama RR. There he formed them in line along a rail fence. On the opposite side of the fence, in the stubble of a mowed meadow, Freeman's Battery became engaged in a duel with one of Negley's batteries which was just out of sight over a hill. An occasional shot would pass in the tree tops over the heads of Starnes' cavalrymen, indicating that the Federal artillery observers must have been able to see them. With the exception of the rearing and plunging of their frightened mounts, the recruits sat in their saddles like veterans.

After about half an hour of watching the cannonading, a Federal percussion shell struck a corner of the fence about the middle of Company "C's" line and exploded, throwing rails high in the air. About a hundred of the Company's new recruits rode hell-bent down the hill toward the railroad bridge. The main support piers of the bridge were only about eight feet apart, and thus prevented the recruits from riding through them as fast as they would have liked. Some galloped along the railroad until they could find a place to cross over.

After an hour of artillery dueling, the Federals began to fall back down the Franklin Pike toward Nashville. Forrest then ordered a cavalry charge, causing the Federals to retreat, while his guns continued to fire from a commanding position on the pike. The Confederates followed for about a mile until the artillery ammunition gave out and a withdrawal to camp was ordered. Forrest reported his losses from the Franklin Pike action as one killed and three wounded.

Pvt. Dan Baird of Company "C" said that just as they turned to form in columns of twos, an extremely handsome boy of about 18 near him, but not of company "C," fell from his horse. At that time there had been no small arms firing heard, and the troops were mystified as to where the minie ball had come from. Baird dismounted to help the boy's two comrades place him back on his horse.

That night a soldier came to Baird and asked how badly hurt he thought the young man was. Baird said he thought he would die. The stranger asked Baird if he had seen the wound. "No," he replied, "but I saw the death pallor on his face." The other friend of the wounded man said that he didn't think he would die because the lady nurse at the field hospital had told him that he was resting quietly, and the doctors had said he was doing as well as could be expected. The two comrades of the boy went to see him at the hospital early the next morning and he was dead.

Most of the people in Nashville, including Military Gov. Johnson who was seen rushing to army headquarters on High Street when Forrest's field guns first opened, had thought the Confederates were coming to try to take the city. The rumors and fears of late June and early July seemed to have come to pass. Forrest, Morgan and Starnes were all involved in a combined move on Nashville. But these commands had been severely depleted in strength and effectiveness by Bragg's and Smith's invasion of Kentucky. They were desperately trying to recruit and rebuild their forces. This demonstration of force by Forrest, supported by infantry to confuse and distract the Federals from Morgan's intended destruction of the railroad station and yard on the opposite side of the river, was about all the strength they could muster.

Despite his night move for an early morning surprise attack, Morgan encountered stubborn resistance and accomplished very little. He managed

FORT ON St CLOUD HILL, NASHVILLE, TENN.
IN COURSE OF CONSTRUCTION, OCT. 15TH '62.

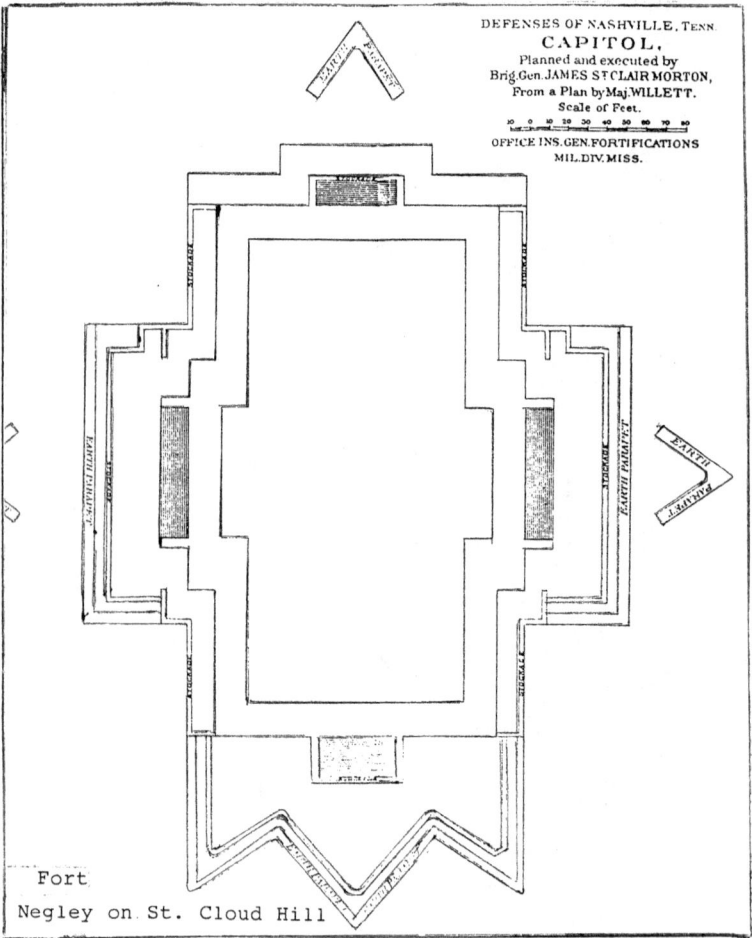

DEFENSES OF NASHVILLE, TENN.
CAPITOL.
Planned and executed by
Brig.Gen.JAMES St CLAIR MORTON,
From a Plan by Maj.WILLETT.
Scale of Feet.

OFFICE INS.GEN.FORTIFICATIONS
MIL.DIV.MISS.

Fort
Negley on St. Cloud Hill

to burn eight rail cars, the station and a machine shop before retreating back to Gallatin. All the firing and noise of battle from the southern perimeter did not distract the "Abolitionists" from concentrating on the defense of Edgefield.

When Starnes' troopers filed back into camp, they found that some 20 to 30 of Company "C's" frightened recruits, in escaping from the shell burst on the rail fence, had kept right on riding past La Vergne for home in Wilson County. Veteran troopers rode out and brought them all back. No disciplinary action of any measure was taken against the deserting recruits, not even verbal admonition or redress by the officers. The troopers, however, took them to task in "unmerciful guying." They said those scared boys went home and spread a report all over the upper part of Wilson County that "the Southern Confederacy was whipped, the army had gone to damnation and the bow-wows," and that "there were a millon Yankees in Nashville and everyone of them carries a double-barreled, self-cocking cannon."

These recruits were assigned or voluntarily attached themselves to companies where they had friends or relatives or both. There were 15 of the Bass family in Company "C" and a total of 20 in Starnes' regiment. Many of them were never formally sworn into Confederate service.

The troops complained that they were having a hard time of it doing picket and outpost duty south of Nashville. Food for the men and forage for the animals were plentiful, and discipline very relaxed. Company officers were called by their first names or nicknames in camp when off duty, and would sign a pass for a private for a day or two off, to go see his girl or go visit a friend or relative to get a good, home-cooked dinner. Even Col. Starnes and Gen. Forrest would countersign a private's pass upon any such reasonable request, if there were no plan or threat of military action. The most distasteful duty for most of the cavalrymen was camp guard duty. They preferred to be on scout or picket, even if there were a chance of a fight every day. This brief period was soon over and everyone of them was to learn, from the months of campaigning ahead, just how good they had had it in the autumn of 1862 in Middle Tennessee.

Word of Pvt. Dan Baird's ability to determine whether or not a wound was fatal spread throughout the regiment. Regimental Surgeon, Dr. Edward Swanson, heard of this reputation, which Baird said brought him "into bad repute with our chief surgeon." A short time later, a 16-year-old recruit named Grandstaff was on camp guard duty with Baird. The young man, out of boredom, set the butt of his shot gun on a low stump and was twirling it around when it slipped off the edge. The hammers struck the top of the stump and the piece discharged one or both barrels through his right shoulder. Baird was nearby and one of the first to reach the boy. Dr. Swanson and his assistant, Allen G. Gooch, came quickly and dressed the wounds where the lad had fallen. They then had him taken to a house close by where he could receive care.

The next day the boy's older brother, Lt. D.W. Grandstaff, overcome with grief, came to Baird and said there was a wagon in camp from his home neighborhood, and if he knew his brother was going to die, he could hold it over until the next day and quickly send the body home for burial by friends without difficulty or cost. Under the circumstances Baird was reluctant to voice an opinion. Tears were streaming down the young lieutenant's face as he begged for a candid opinion, saying that this was his only brother and his mother's pride. For quite awhile Baird remained silent and then said, "Lieutenant sir, hold the wagon until tomorrow," saluted and walked away.

Dr. Swanson heard about the conversation and searched out Pvt. Baird. The doctor's reputation was that of "an exceedingly hot tempered man and the most comprehensive, exhaustive, and fluent cusser in Forrest's entire command." After administering a complete "cussing out" of Baird, the doctor assured Lt. Grandstaff that his brother had a fair chance of survival. The wagon was released to return home and the boy, Pvt. Grandstaff of Company "C," died the following day.

A week after the demonstration against Nashville, the main, western Confederate army arrived back in Middle Tennessee. Gen. Bragg set up headquarters at Tullahoma and again assumed command of all operations. On November 30, 1862, a month after 26-year-old "Little Joe" Wheeler was commissioned Brig. General, Bragg placed him in command of all his five brigades of cavalry. Bragg referred to three of these as regular brigades; the other two ,Forrest's and Morgan's, he regarded as fit only for partisan activity, such as conducting raids on enemy lines of supply and communication.

The Union army was massing again in Nashville under Maj. Gen. William S. Rosecrans. Grant was advancing his army from West Tennessee on Vicksburg. His line of supply was to be the railroads from Columbus, Kentucky to northern Mississippi.

John C. Pemberton had recently been promoted to Lieutenant General and given command of the Confederate Dept. of Mississippi, Tennessee and Eastern Louisiana. Recognizing the inadequacy of his forces in defending against the Union advance, he appealed to Gen. Bragg for help. On November 21st Bragg responded by wire that he would send a large cavalry force under Forrest into West Tennessee to create a diversion and disrupt Grant's line of supply. About the first of December, Forrest's command was ordered to Columbia, Tennessee to prepare for this operation.

Forrest expressed his strong objections to operating deep into enemy-held territory with poorly-armed recruits, and made application to Bragg for arms. No arms, supplies or reinforcements were sent to Columbia, and on December 10th Bragg impatiently ordered Forrest to move at once. The next day Col. Starnes put his regiment in line of march on the Mt. Pleasant road, and then on the road to Lawrenceberg, Tennessee.

CAPITOL HILL FORTIFIED—Andrew Johnson, military governor (and future President) thundered defiance from behind its Yankee stockade. (from the Nashville Banner)

Forrest's Raid Into West Tennessee

Starnes' 4th Cavalry Regiment arrived at Clifton, Tennessee on the Tennessee River on the 15th. They turned off to the north side of the road and "bivouacked in the bushes without fires." The command did not want to attract the attention of the Federal gunboats known to be patrolling the river. During the night they were moved onto a low bluff close to the river's edge.

A little beyond the middle of the river was Wright's Island, not much more than a large sand and gravel bar, on which the advance men built two or three large fires and assembled some horses. By companies the troopers removed their saddles, tied their overcoats, blankets and personal belongings into bundles as compact as possible, which were then ferried with them out to the island by canoes. The horses were pushed off the bluff for about a ten-foot free fall into the cold, swift and rising current. They would disappear in the river, and when they surfaced, the poor, confused animals would swim in circles until one saw the horses at the fires on the sandbar and struck out for them. Some followed, but others never saw the firelight and exhausted themselves trying to climb up the steep bank over which they had been pushed. Losses were high, about six to ten of each company's mounts.

A cold, drizzling rain was falling as the men stood on the island waiting to form for transport to the west side of the river. It took about two hours before the order came down for Company "C" to mount up and ride to the north end of the island. By that time every man was soaked to the skin. Forrest's vanguard of carpenters and others had earlier built and hidden two large flatboats, which were now used to ferry men and horses to the enemy-held side of the river. Twenty-five men and horses at a time could be carried by these boats. It was broad daylight when some of Starnes' men reached the temporary camp that the advance contingent had set up on the riverbank. But it took from the 15th through the 17th to transport Forrest's whole command across the river and regroup it for the advance on Union-held posts in West Tennessee.

From Gen. Forrest to the rawest recruit, everyone knew they were in a potential trap between the Mississippi and Tennessee Rivers, which converge to the north in Union-held Kentucky, and Grant's army was to the south. And there were several areas that were well-garrisoned and patrolled by the Federals along their planned line of attack to destroy the railroads. There was a deep feeling throughout the command that perhaps the brigade was to be sacrificed by drawing off large Union forces in order to save Pemberton's 20,000 plus Rebels at Vicksburg.

The troops under Forrest's command for this raid were: Starnes' Fourth, Dibrell's Eighth, Biffle's Ninth Tennessee and Russell's Fourth Alabama Regiments, Maj. Nicholas N. Cox's Tennessee Battalion, Maj. Thomas G. Woodward's two companies of Kentuckians, Capt. Bill Forrest's scouts, and Capt. Montgomery W. Little's company of Gen. Forrest's escort. In all they numbered about 2,100 cavalrymen, supported by Capt. Samuel L. Freeman's Battery of six brass howitzers and one other piece. Poorly armed and outfitted, there were no more than 1,500 or 1,600 effectives in the command. The brigade camped eight miles west of the river on the night of December 17th.

Five miles out of Lexington, Tennessee at Beech Creek on the morning of December 18th, a Federal battery, concealed in the cane on the banks of the creek, opened fire on the twenty-man advance of Russell's Alabamians who were leading the column.   The Union forces of 773 were under the command of Col. Robert G. Ingersoll of the 11th Illinois Cavalry, which also included men of the 14th Indiana Battery of two steel Rodmans, the 2nd West Tennessee and 5th Ohio Cavalry regiments.

Capt. Freeman wheeled his artillery up to the bridge, but found the floor planking had been removed. Details from Starnes' 4th Regiment took down a snake-rail fence nearby, and quickly refloored the bridge with rails. Protected by Starnes, the artillery guns and caissons rolled across. Biffle and Dibrell moved their regiments over another road where the bridge had not been destroyed, as Col. Ingersoll had ordered. With Capt. Gurley leading four companies of the 4th Alabama, they broke the left and right of Ingersoll's line, leaving him and his 11th Illinois and the battery on their own. The battery was well protected and they and the Illinois cavalry fought hard. Forrest then ordered Captain Charles W. Anderson, of his staff, to make a circuit with Gurley and 250 men to the enemy's rear. Starnes and Dibrell, in support of the artillery, put up such a show of fight on the front that Anderson and Gurley were within 150 yards of them before the 11th Illinois were aware of their advance. The last shot fired by Col. Ingersoll's battery, as the Rebel charge reached the guns, disintegrated Alabamian 1st Sgt. J.L.P. Kelly and his horse.

About this time the last of Starnes' men got across Beech Creek and were ordered to shoot the men who were cutting the harness of the enemy artillery horses. That they did, but accidentally wounded some of the horses they wanted to capture. Capt. Frank Gurley of the 4th Alabama captured the two guns and was joined by Col. Starnes in chasing Col. Ingersoll and his cavalry.

They found the Illinois colonel, who was later to become a nationally known, agnostic lecturer and writer, hiding under the porch of a house. Some difficulty was encountered in getting Col. Ingersoll to come out and surrender. Starnes and Gurley didn't want to shoot under the porch or to wound or kill the Yankee colonel. Finally they coaxed him out and Gurley accepted his surrender. They took him to Gen. Forrest, who was very impressed with the intelligence and dignity of this man, and paroled him on the spot. This skirmish at a slough in West Tennessee ended the colonel's military career.

Col. Starnes pursued the portion of Col. Ingersoll's command who were trying to escape to their main garrison in Jackson. He picked up stragglers and a good number of arms. Forrest's Brigade reached the vicinity of Jackson on the afternoon of the 18th and drove the enemy picket forces into their works.

Forrest sent Dibrell north to destroy the Mobile & Ohio Railroad at Carroll Station. The 4th Alabama Regiment and the 2nd Tennessee Battalion, under Col. Russell and Maj. Cox, were ordered south of Jackson to destroy the bridge, culverts and trestles on the railroads that ran from the city to Bolivar, Tennessee and Corinth, Mississippi. The rest of the brigade went into camp about five miles out on the Lexington road. Big campfires were built as an element of Forrest's show of a big force.

Brig. Gen. Jeremiah C. Sullivan ordered Col. Adolph Engelman, with his 43rd and the 61st Illinois regiments of infantry, out to join and take command of any and all Union cavalry that he might find, and to "feel the enemy." About 9:30 PM they came upon what was left of Ingersoll's cavalry, and a mile and a half farther they could see the big, bright campfires of the Rebel cavalry. Col. Engelman thought of attacking, but was reminded by his subordinate commanders that night attacks are always hazardous and should only be attempted where the attackers are "perfectly acquainted with the country." The Federals shivered in the extremely cold night as they watched the glowing fires from the comfortable Rebel encampment. Col. Engelman was concerned about the men's comfort, but felt it "prudent to prohibit the kindling of any fire."

At daybreak on Friday, December 19, 1862 Forrest advanced with only the regiments of Starnes and Biffle, Maj. T.J. Woodward's two companies of Kentuckians, and Freeman's Battery. Col. Engelman's 11th Illinois Cavalry, armed with carbines, waited for them on the bluff of the branch that ran through the Brooks farm. Starnes' and Biffle's details casually reconnoitered the position, drawing a few long-range shots to determine the disposition of the enemy. Then Freeman's Battery and the two captured Rodmans, which Forrest had assigned to Lt. John Morton, opened a crossfire on the hapless Illinois cavalry and drove them back to a second defensive position near the Salem Cemetery.

Biffle's and Starnes' cavalries advanced slowly up the road at a trot-walk, then a trot and then, with a rebel yell, charged at full gallop on the center of the enemy line. They were met with a well-directed fire which caused momentary confusion as the leaders turned back into the other cavalry advancing behind them. Having now learned the position of Col. Engelman's infantry, Forrest's batteries advanced while the cavalry made demonstrations against both his flanks. Some pieces were placed on the high

Col. Engelman fell back to Jackson. After having made a show of force, Forrest observed that the garrison was definitely taking up a defensive position and preparing for an assault. Between four and five in the afternoon, almost sundown at that time of year, Forrest cautiously moved to Spring Creek. With Col. Russell's regiment guarding the rear, Dibrell was ordered to destroy the bridge and stockade at Forked Deer Creek. Biffle was to get to the rear of Trenton, while Forrest attacked frontally with Cox's battalion and Freeman's battery. Col. Starnes was sent to take Humboldt, Tennessee.

Forrest used every conceivable means of spreading an exaggeration of the number of troops in his command, to the extent of involving the private soldiers in the deception. Many good women among the friendly citizenry came out to their front gates with whatever tasty foods they may have cooked and offered them to the perpetually hungry troopers. One such lady inquired as to how many troops "Mr. Forrest" had. Tom Jones, a lanky private in Starnes' regiment, asked her if she knew how many trees there were standing in West Tennessee. When she replied that she certainly did not, he told her that Forrest had enough men to put one behind every tree, and two or three behind the largest ones.

Starnes arrived at Humboldt around noon on December 20, 1862, and promptly began an assault on the garrison. Most of the garrison's effectives had been ordered to the defense of Jackson. The convalescents and others made a brief attempt to defend the place, and then tried to burn the magazine. By 1 PM or a little after, they had surrendered. More than 100 prisoners, 500 stands of arms, 300,000 rounds of small arms ammunition and a large supply of artillery harnesses and government stores were captured. One of the 4th Tennessee's troopers played a tune on an appropriated fiddle while his comrades danced on the captured colors of "D" Company, 122nd Illinois Infantry.

Meanwhile Pvt. Dan Baird had become separated from his regiment and, observing some Confederates trying to capture the Federal blockhouse at Forked Deer Creek, dismounted and joined them. But he found they were from Dibrell's regiment and that his regiment had been ordered to Humboldt. He remounted and rode as fast as his horse could travel toward that place. About four miles from the town, Baird heard cannonading and then an increasing artillery fire. The returning private judged that Starnes' regiment "had cut off more than it could masticate." He found, on his arrival, that the shell explosions he had heard were from the burning of large ordnance stores.

All the stores and ordnance that could not be carried away were burned in "a magnificent, daylight fireworks display." Pieces of shells, warehouses, chunks of fire and clouds of smoke and ashes were flying in all directions. Sgt. Tom Tulloss said that the rest of the day and most of the night were spent in burning the railroad station, tearing up the track and destroying the trestles. He was proud of carrying off 500 new Enfield rifles.

Baird got "two new Union six-shooters" and turned in his two old ones to the ordnance sergeant. They got a little sleep that night and a little rest the next morning. When Starnes arrived in the Trenton area early in the afternoon, he found that Forrest had captured the garrison, burned all the military stores he could not transport and moved north toward Union City. Forrest had also paroled the Federals taken prisoner and allowed Col. Jacob Fry to keep his sword since it was a family heirloom. The large number of prisoners had become a problem to guard and an encumbrance to the movement of Forrest's raid; about 1300 were paroled.

Privates Tom Jones and Dan Baird had been living on canned strawberries, crackers and a concoction they called "Otard Brandy," most of which they admitted was stolen. Now their stocks were running low. The three proprietors of a nearby large sutlers store refused to accept Confederate "script" as a medium of exchange and locked their doors. Jones took about a dozen troopers and went to "remonstrate" with them about the unfairness of their business practices.

While Jones was "remonstrating" with the owners in front of the store, there was a loud crash as the back door was broken down. One of the proprietors unlocked the front door, rushed in, collared a big cavalryman and hit him in the face. Almost instantly a shelf board was split in half over his head, rendering him unconscious. In a few minutes the store was filled with Starnes' armed and angry cavalrymen. Word had gone out that the sutlers had killed a soldier. The store shelves were completely bare in a matter of minutes.

Among the loot taken was a large quantity of interest-bearing Confederate notes. Pvt. Tom "Granny" Bass said there were "dead oodles" of counterfeit money. They knew it was counterfeit because the printing and paper was far superior to any Confederate money any of the troopers had ever seen. It was as good as gold for playing poker, if they ever got time for a game on this expedition.

Forrest's force continued the destruction of the Mobile & Ohio Railroad northward, striking, in turn, Rutherford Station and Kenton on December 21st. That evening Starnes rejoined Forrest. When they reached the long, high, wooden trestles of the south and north forks of the Obion River between Kenton and Union City, Starnes men assailed the structures with 500 captured and "pressed" axes. Chips flew from the sleet and ice-coated trestles, but, "the wood was as hard as horn, the axes dull as froes with poor handles." Pvt. Baird, the unofficial judge of whether a wound was mortal or not, was one of the squad leaders. Lt. Col. T. J. Woodward asked about the progress being made in destroying the trestle structures. Baird took credit for presenting the idea to Woodward of having half the men cut and split dry kindling while the other half built and tended fires on the top of the trestle at every point where the sills crossed the bents.

The method worked well, and they dropped a mile of trestle on the flooded bottoms by the time darkness fell on Christmas Eve. Forrest had forced the surrender of the Union City garrison on the 23rd, and had torn up the railroad as far as Moscow, Kentucky by the 24th. He then ordered most of his regiments into camp for a Christmas Day rest. Starnes' regiment worked the night of the 24th and the early morning hours of the 25th to complete the destruction of the trestles.

Back in the occupied city of Nashville, a military commission convened on Christmas Day to investigate Maj. Gen. Don Carlos Buell's campaign in Tennessee and Kentucky.

> Question by Gen. Buell: Were the principal depredations... committed by organized troops...?

> Answer by Col. John F. Miller, 29th Indiana Volunteers testifying for the defendant [Gen. Buell]: I do not know whether they were organized or not; I know they were in the Confederate service; they were understood to be guerrillas. We knew them to be the forces under Morgan, Forrest and Starnes.

During the cross-examination of the witness by Judge Advocate, Maj. Donn Piatt:

> Question by Brig. Gen. Daniel Tyler, USV, a member of the commission: Do you think these parties of guerrillas, as you term them, had any direct assistance from the people...?

> Gen. Buell: I object to this term "guerrillas" as applied to these troops. They are as much troops as any in rebel service. There is a difference between the cavalry of Morgan, Forrest and Starnes and what we understand by "guerrillas." I know of no reason for giving them a character which does not belong to them, for they are not "guerrillas" in the proper sense of that term.

Brig. Gen. Thomas Davies, USV, commanding the Federal District at Columbus, Kentucky, whose forces outnumbered Forrest's by two to one, had been sent into a state of panic by the Confederate advance. He requested reinforcements to defend against an attack on Columbus. When Grant, who knew how to fight Forrest, ordered Davies not to wait for Forrest to attack, but to go out and fight him, Davies appealed by wire to Washington. Maj. Gen. Henry Halleck overruled Grant. Reinforcements were ordered to Davies from St. Louis and Cairo. He reported to Halleck on December 24th, "Cheatham has crossed the Tennessee with 40,000 men and is marching north. I cannot hold Columbus against that force."

To avoid the Federals under Brig. Gen. I.N. Haynie, who had reached Trenton, the Confederate brigade moved southeast from Union City to Dresden, tearing up the Paducah branch of the railroad. The road had been cut up and rutted by the wagons and was frozen hard; "... our horses were half dead with starvation and exposure." Starnes' regiment arrived before dark with the main column on December 26th.

On the 27th the brigade moved 15 miles to McKenzie. Here Gen. Forrest was advised that two infantry brigades were moving to intercept him. All the bridges across the South Fork of the Obion on their front had been destroyed, and all crossings were under heavy Union guard. At noon, about nine miles from the main force, Starnes halted his men for a rest at a crossroad leading from McKenzie to Huntingdon . A Union patrol of about 80 cavalrymen came upon them from the direction of Huntingdon and opened fire. Col. Starnes formed a line of battle, then led the attack when the first volley turned the Federal advance into a hasty retreat. Pvt. Dan Baird had fed his horse, and was fast asleep on a bush near the road with his shotgun cradled in his arms, when he "awoke amid the most infernal din of firearms, clattering of horses feet and yells." When the Yankees went flying by him in retreat, he fired both barrels at them from a distance of only 20 feet with no visible effect. He reloaded and capped his gun with fingers so cold he could not feel the caps, mounted and galloped with the others after the fleeing Yankees. They found "one dead Yankee on the road," Pvt. Anderson Hagar, Company "C," and another seriously wounded man coming back. The very bloody man with Hagar said, "Boy's we whipped them but they got me." Andy Hagar was shot through the lungs and bleeding from his mouth.   Baird decided via his "death pallor theory" that neither man was mortally wounded; neither died.

Col. Starnes was with his old company "F" when the Yankees opened fire and he ordered them to mount and lead the charge, and to crowd them until they came upon the main Union force. Lt. John Norris and Sgt. Tom Tulloss happened to get some distance in front of their pursuing company and came right upon the Yankee infantry lying on the ground within 20 or 30 yards of them. An officer ordered them to surrender. They wheeled and ran. Norris' horse was killed and Tulloss' mare was shot through the lower left ear. Lt. Norris grabbed the sergeant's left stirrup, eventually got up behind him and made it out of rifle range without either being hit.

Forrest's force left McKenzie Station the morning of the 28th. At sundown on the sluggish South Fork of the Obion, halfway between the hamlet of McLemoresville and Huntingdon, Starnes' regiment, with the rest of Forrest's brigade, except Dibrell's and Cox's commands who were watching the flanks and rear, drew up at an old bridge. This old double bridge was so deteriorated that Sullivan's Union forces did not think it passable, even for pedestrians. Its flooring was rotted and the causeways leading up to it on both sides of the stream were bogs of mire for a quarter mile.

Ten men from Starnes' and each of the other regiments were soon set to cutting forked timbers from the swamp trees to shore up the bridge timbers and trestles. The General was a "full hand" among the men, wielding an axe.

A cold drizzle was falling in the misty dusk of a winter evening lighted by the glow of torches and candles. In an hour or so, the bridge had been repaired to the extent that it allowed some cavalry to cross. But crossing with the heavy-laden wagons and artillery was another matter that caused some reluctance to chance it with a team of horses. Forrest climbed into the driver's seat of one of his headquarters wagons and drove it across the bridge as an example of confidence that it could be done. The next two drivers of ammunition wagons were not so fortunate, and were upset into the cold, muddy river. Officers as well as the men were badly discouraged. "Old Forrest's" vicious temper flared and there was an outburst of profanity in the evening gloom. Men waded into the numbing cold of the stream, and under such exposure and with great effort, the wagons were righted and pulled out on the opposite bank.

Five hundred men and their officers were ordered up to repair the bridge and assist the wagons in crossing. By 3 AM on the 29th, the twenty-nine wagons of the train were across. Fifty men were assigned to each gun as it came the artillery's turn to cross. Three hours more of pushing, pulling, cursing, and whipping the horses, men's backs against the gun-carriage wheels, brought the battery over the Obion.

The night of the 27th, Col. Cyrus Dunham's 1800-man infantry brigade had marched at 11 PM from Trenton eastward toward them. Col. John W. Fuller's brigade of 2,000 marched at daybreak on the 28th to follow Dunham toward Huntingdon with generals Sullivan and Haynie.

Forrest was now between two heavy brigades of the enemy and knew full well that everyone of those guns was going to be needed.

Gen. Haynie believed that Forrest, in such a tight spot, would head directly east to the Tennessee River. Brig. Gen. G.M. Dodge had been ordered up from Corinth, Mississippi with two heavy infantry brigades, cavalry and artillery, to cut off the Confederate escape route toward Clifton. Shortly after the rear of Sullivan's force had marched through McLemoresville on their way to Huntingdon, the vanguard of Forrest's tired column emerged from the swampy bottoms and entered the village on the 29th. That evening Dunham's and Fuller's brigades reached Huntingdon.

Forrest stayed in camp all day December 30th, resting his men and their horses. From this encampment at Flake's Store to the rear of the Union position, 15 miles from Lexington, he could make a run for the Tennessee River. But a heavily-contested crossing under fire would place his command in even more jeopardy. While Forrest's men rested, Dunham moved back to Clarksburg by a forced march.

That evening the General sent out his younger brother, Bill Forrest, and his independent company of men that the boys called "the forty thieves," to attract Dunham's attention and draw him into a fight before Fuller's brigade could come to his support. Starnes went out on a scouting mission. Finding the Rebels only four miles away, Dunham sent a message to Sullivan and Haynie suggesting that they move to his aid. Early the next morning he moved toward a place known as Parker's Crossroads, where the roads from McLemoresville and Clarksburg crossed at an angle. On arriving in front of the Rev. John Parker's home, Col. Dunham began to place his battery of three pieces there. The Reverend, who until this time had been a Union sympathizer, strongly, but unsuccessfully, protested that if Dunham fired from this position, the Rebels would certainly fire back and destroy his home.

Earlier that morning of the 31st, Capt. McLemore, of Starnes' regiment, was sent out with four companies for the purpose of getting to the rear of Dunham's brigade and taking the road to Clarksburg and Huntingdon in order to protect the Confederate rear against any unexpected arrival of Sullivan with Fuller's brigade. Starnes took his regiment out early on a foraging mission in the direction of Huntingdon, where there was a brief clash with Federal cavalry.

As Dunham, in line of battle, intercepted the Confederate march toward Lexington at Hicks Field, Forrest opened on him with grape and canister from one howitzer gun under Lt. Nat Baxter, Jr. Dunham responded with his 7th Wisconsin Battery. In half an hour seven guns under Capt. Freeman and Lt. Morton wheeled up on each side of Baxter's piece and opened a devastating fire on the Federal infantry. At 9 AM Dunham withdrew to a position three quarters of a mile southeast of Parker's Crossroads.

During the morning, Forrest continued the pressure on the Yankees, fighting mostly with his artillery, and supported by Russell's and Dibrell's dismounted men. Col. Starnes heard the firing nine miles from Parker's Crossroads. He put his regiment at the run all the way back to the crossroads, which was accomplished within an hour to arrive a little before noon. They passed Cox's horse holders and rode through his men who were in line of battle in support of Freeman's Battery. Gen. Forrest met Starnes at the battery and said, "Colonel move around behind them. I've got them going; charge them at once."

Starnes went westward around the left flank of Dunham's line and charged into the flank of the 39th Iowa Infantry. Col. H.J.B. Cummings' men staggered under Starnes' fire, but rallied in a strong fight as they fell back. Col. Cummings reported that he was reforming his men, who were retreating from the murderous artillery fire, "when we were opened upon by a heavy fire of dismounted men who had advanced under the cover of thick underbrush to within 50 feet of my men."

Forrest ordered the fire redoubled on the Union line. Flying splinters from the cedar rails, behind which they were lying, killed and wounded several of the 39th Iowa, causing them to break across the road to reform in a cornfield. Their losses were three killed, 33 wounded and 11 missing.

Col. Alonzo Napier, who had joined Forrest at Trenton on the evening of the 20th with 430 troopers, led his men in a charge ordered by Forrest, to break the Union lines near Starnes' position. He was killed while standing on top of a rail fence, urging his men forward. And a number of his men were killed in this expensive charge on the Yankees behind the rail fence. It did succeed in pushing back the enemy lines rapidly enough to cause the abandonment of their remaining two guns. Dunham was now without wagons or artillery, and surrounded on three sides. White flags began to appear.

Forrest, thinking he had the roads covered, ordered a cease-fire, and sent forward a flag of truce and a demand for surrender. The firing ceased for about 15 minutes while Dunham considered the demand. He tried to negotiate via a counter offer to allow Forrest to withdraw without pursuit or further fighting, while playing for time and hoping Sullivan would arrive. Then there was a heavy burst of musketry from the direction of Parker's house at the Confederate rear.

Fuller's Brigade struck Maj. N.N. Cox's horse holders, then his battalion of 250. They put up a good fight and slowed the advance enough to give Forrest a little time to assess the situation and take some action to save his brigade. Maj. Cox and his battalion were all captured.

When informed by Col. Charles Carroll of his staff that a heavy line of infantry was attacking their rear, Forrest issued his famous "Charge them both ways!" order. But it was the two former physicians, Starnes and Russell, who heard the firing and sensed Forrest's predicament of being caught between two brigades. Without orders, they attacked Dunham so fiercely that not a single shot was fired from that brigade in the direction of any other of Forrest's forces on the field. By an aggressive show of force made by the Confederates he could quickly gather up, many of whom were unhorsed and unarmed, Forrest convinced Gen. Sullivan that he was outnumbered and would probably be attacked as soon as they could regroup. The ever cautious Sullivan went into a defensive position and made no attempt to pursue the fleeing Rebels. Starnes fell back from Dunham's front and awaited orders. Forrest told him to take the lead toward Lexington with his 4th Tennessee.

Lt. John Morton rode beside Gen. Forrest as they quit the field of battle. The General could not understand the surprise attack or what might

Col. Dunham's Infantry moves out early in the morning to intercept Forrest at Parker's Crossroads (Reenactment)

Forrest opens fire on Dunham's Brigade with his first three pieces of artillery (Reenactment)

A company of Starnes' dismounted men fire into the flank of the 39th Iowa Infantry (Reenactment)

Gen. Forrest rides up to tell Col Starnes to lead the cavalry column out from Parker's Crossroads toward Lexington (Reenactment)

have happened to Capt. McLemore and his four companies. It just did not seem possible that the Yankees could have killed or captured everyone of the detachment. As it turned out, his written instructions for McLemore, given to Starnes, were very vague, so vague that both officers interpreted them to mean a reconnaissance, and not the posting of a heavy-picket guard on the road, as intended. Therefore, McLemore had moved on the flank of Haynie, Fuller and Sullivan's advance, rather than in front of it.

When Brig. Generals Sullivan and Haynie were riding with their staffs toward Clarksburg, they saw some of Capt. McLemore's men and veered eastward off the road into the woods to avoid capture; they were not detected. McLemore heard Dunham's guns firing and attempted to return to help his regiment, unaware of leaving the road open for an attack on Forrest's rear. He did not know where Starnes' regiment was or that Starnes, too, had heard the firing and was hurrying back to Forrest. Later in the morning south of Clarksburg, Fuller's advance saw McLemore's detachment filing westwardly off the road and into some woods.

The day was one of multiple misfortunes for Capt. McLemore. He had missed a chance to capture two Yankee generals, did not intercept the enemy advance and did not catch up with his regiment. All this occurred twenty miles or so from the West Tennessee settlement named for his family.

About a mile south of Parker's Crossroads, a body of cavalry was seen coming toward Starnes' regiment. The distance was too great to tell who they were. Col. Starnes was sure they were Yankees and ordered his Company "F," under the command of Lt. J.T. Pierce, forward to meet them. Lt. John Norris was still riding behind Sgt. Tulloss.

"John, drop off here," the sergeant said, "If they are Yankees , I will sure get you a horse."

In five minutes it was ascertained that the cavalrymen were the enemy and Lt. Pierce ordered a charge. The Federals held their ground until Starnes' men were nearly on them, and then broke in confusion. About fifty were captured and all were very well mounted. Sgt. Tulloss ran up to the Lieutenant in command and took his "splendid horse" for Lt. Norris. The grateful Norris rode that horse during the rest of the war. The Yankee Lieutenant may have been D.S. Scott of the 11th Illinois Cavalry, who was reported captured by Col. Dunham.

Forrest moved 12 miles from the Parker's Crossroads Battlefield to camp at Lexington, treat the wounded and rest, on the night of December 31, 1862. About 2 AM, New Year's morning of 1863, the order was given to mount up and head for the Tennessee River. Ten miles east of Lexington at daylight, Starnes' men and the others, except Dibrell's regiment who were sent ahead, were allowed a three-hour rest; the prisoners were paroled.

Shortly after moving out again, the advance men reported that a heavy line of Federal cavalry was blocking the road toward the river. It was known that Brig. Gen. G.M. Dodge was moving up from Corinth and Purdy with two brigades of infantry, supported by artillery and cavalry, to get between Forrest and his river-crossing-point at Clifton.

The pickets of Lt. Col. William K.M. Breckenridge's 6th Tennessee regiment of Union cavalry were driven in, and an attempt was made to form a defensive line of battle on a hill. Then they fell back to another position. Forrest did not bother to reconnoiter the Federals and ordered Dibrell to charge the center, Biffle the right and sent Starnes to the left. This movement quickly scattered the Union Tennessee cavalry, and the rebels continued their rapid ride to the west bank of the Tennessee River. They arrived between noon and 1 PM.

The two flatboats used to cross the river on the way westward had been raised from their hiding place on the east bank and brought over to the other side. Artillery pieces and artillerists, ammunition and supply wagons were ferried over first. There was no time to transport the horses by boat. Starnes troopers removed the saddles, bridles and packs their horses were carrying and pushed the critters into the stream, forcing them to swim across following the swimming, lead animals being held by men in skiffs. Saddles and equipment were brought over by boat. By 10 AM on January 2, 1863, Forrest's command was on the east bank.

Gen. Sullivan had sent Col. Michael Lawler, 18th Illinois Infantry, with 3,000 men, his brigade from Jackson and Col. Fuller's from Lexington, in pursuit on new Year's Day. During the morning of January 3rd they arrived opposite Clifton and deployed along the west riverbank and in the nearby timber. When the Union cavalry appeared, Forrest's artillery pieces, posted on the higher banks on the east side of the Tennessee River, opened fire on them. A four-hour skirmish followed between the Rebel artillerists and the Union infantry, who were trying to pick them off from across the river. The Federals didn't see any enemy other than the artillery, and could not use their batteries effectively because of the high banks opposite them, and made no effort to do so.

A sergeant summed up the fifteen days in West Tennessee:

Starnes' men all had new guns, many good pistols and to a man they had new army saddles and bridles and good woolen blankets that we got in Humboldt. In a few days we were back at Columbia and Spring Hill.

Alabama Pvt. J.R. Harris described the raid through West Tennessee:

We captured Lexington, Humboldt and Trenton... got Gen. [Col.] Fry and Bob Ingersoll. We had won the fight at Parker's Crossroads and the Yankees were stacking their arms when the yell of 'Reinforcements' was heard. They then grabbed guns again and we were forced to retreat.

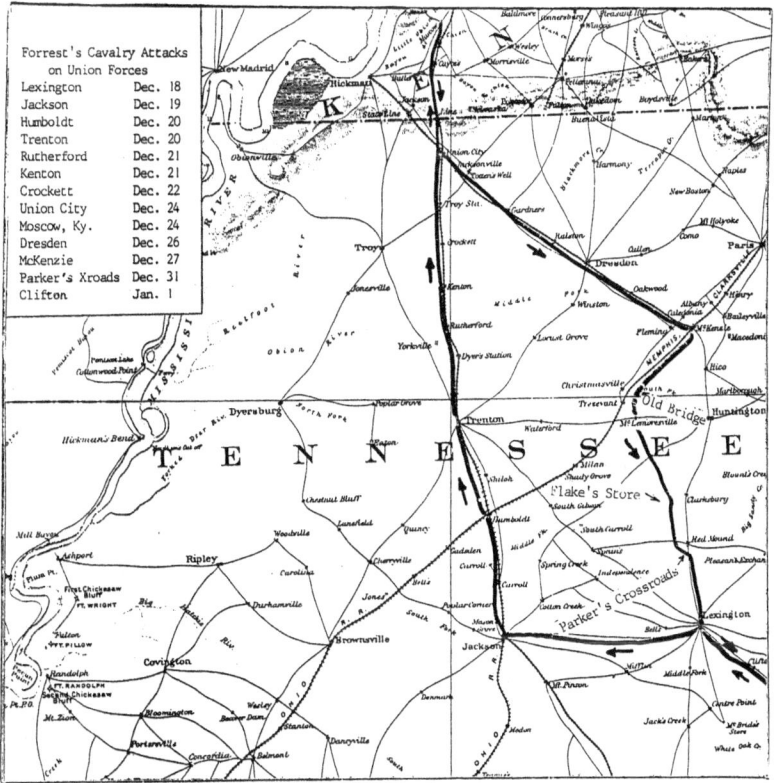

Forrest's Second Raid, Dec. 11, 1862 - Jan. 3, 1863

Fort Donelson

When Starnes' 4th Tennessee reached Columbia, Tennessee, they found that the second most famous cavalryman in Tennessee, Brig. Gen. John H. Morgan, had been on his third raid into Kentucky, avoided a large force trying to trap him, and by a night ride had arrived there January 1st. Forrest was considered the most renowned cavalry leader in the state, with Starnes the third, behind Morgan. Another surprise was the news that the day they had crossed the river into West Tennessee with Forrest, Gen. Morgan had wed Miss Mattie Ready in the fanciest Confederate ceremony yet. Pres. Jefferson Davis, Gen. Bragg and a host of CSA brass had been in attendance at the nuptials in Murfreesboro. Lt.Gen. Leonidas Polk, an Episcopal bishop, officiated.

After the bloody, indecisive battle of Stones River, December 31, 1862 and January 2, 1863, Union Maj. Gen. William S. Rosecrans had taken up a position at Murfreesboro with his Army of the Cumberland. Bragg's Confederates were concentrated around Shelbyville. From there the new Confederate line ran along behind a broken ridge eastward to Wartrace, just north of the Duck River. Starnes' regiment was on picket and scout duty with Forrest's Brigade, protecting Bragg's extreme left flank. Every night Starnes had scouts in the Yankee lines. This activity continued for three weeks.

Twenty-six-year-old West Pointer, Joseph Wheeler, whom Gen. Bragg had made Chief of Cavalry during the retreat from Kentucky (when Col. Starnes was covering the rear in Col. Scott's brigade), was promoted to Major General in the latter part of January. Thus he became Forrest's commanding officer. Wheeler was ordered to disrupt Union navigation on the Cumberland River downstream of occupied Nashville. He took Brig. Gen. John A. Wharton's brigade, Starnes' regiment and some other commands of Forrest's brigade on this expedition.

Col. John M. Harlan, (10th Kentucky Infantry), commanding a brigade, reported on Saturday night, January 24th, that Rebel cavalry, numbering between 3,000 and 4,000 men, and eight pieces of artillery, came from the direction of Franklin and halted at Concord Church. He stated that the force was Wheeler's and Forest's old brigades, "temporarily under the command of Starnes."

About the end of the month, Wheeler ordered Forrest to take 800 of his men and operate on the Cumberland River to interrupt navigation. Forrest masked his battery and positioned his men in ambush to do battle with any passing Federal boat or barge near Palmyra. Wheeler found that the Federal commanders had become aware of his intentions and had ceased, for the present, all navigation on the river, leaving him nothing to attack. Rather than return to his base with no significant military action to report, Wheeler then decided that an assault could retake Fort Donelson.

Gen. Bragg then ordered Forrest to follow and take command of his own men. After two days of hard riding he found them shivering in the cold, fifteen miles from Dover, Tennessee. At his insistence, a general inspection was called. Starnes' troopers, like the others of Forrest's command, had only 15 rounds of ammunition each, and were without sufficient cooking utensils and rations. One of them described the weather as "bad - first rain and then a real big snow." Forrest's protestations against an attack on the garrison of 800 men of the 83rd Illinois Infantry were unheeded, and his brigade arrived in sight of the fort about noon February 3rd.

Wheeler thought that a quick assault from both sides of the fortification could take it without significant losses, and ordered an immediate dismounted advance. The 8th Texas from Wharton's Brigade was sent west out on the road to Fort Henry, on which Federal reinforcements were advancing. Forrest's forces were dismounted and deployed on the east side, Wharton's understrength brigade to the west and southwest. A flag of truce was sent in and an unconditional surrender was demanded. Surrender was declined by the Colonel commanding the garrison, and the Confederate batteries opened on the advanced guns of the fort.

Forrest was directed to wait until Gen. Wheeler got to Wharton's lines where, at a designated time, a general attack would commence. Before Wheeler reached that point and before the attacking battle lines were formed, action began. Mistaking a movement of three or four companies of the enemy toward the river at the double quick for a retreat, Forrest ordered a remount and charge. These men of the 83rd Illinois had been ordered to occupy a deep ravine a short distance beyond their position. Col. Starnes led this charge with Forrest, and when the Federal infantry saw this column of several hundred charging, Rebel cavalrymen, they opened fire and ran back for the breastworks. Forrest and Starnes attempted to ride down and capture these men, or use them as shields and follow them into their works.

However, the distance was short enough for the detachment to get over the embankment and join in the fusillade of small arms, firing into Starnes regiment and the other cavalry in this desperate charge. Grape and canister-loaded siege and field guns fired into the mass of horses and men. Forrest's horse went down and the men thought he was killed. Col.Starnes received a facial wound; horses and men went down in this slaughter. His second-in-command, Lt. Col. Peril C. Haynes, was shot in the mouth, a very severe wound. Lt. Hughes and Orderly Brittain had their horses killed by the same shell. Privates James Scruggs and "Brother" Hunter, a Cumberland preacher of Starnes' old Company "F," were killed instantly. There was no choice but to withdraw due to the casualties taken in this mounted attack.

The troopers were dismounted and reformed as infantry for a second assault, this time in conjunction with Wharton's advance. Using the buildings

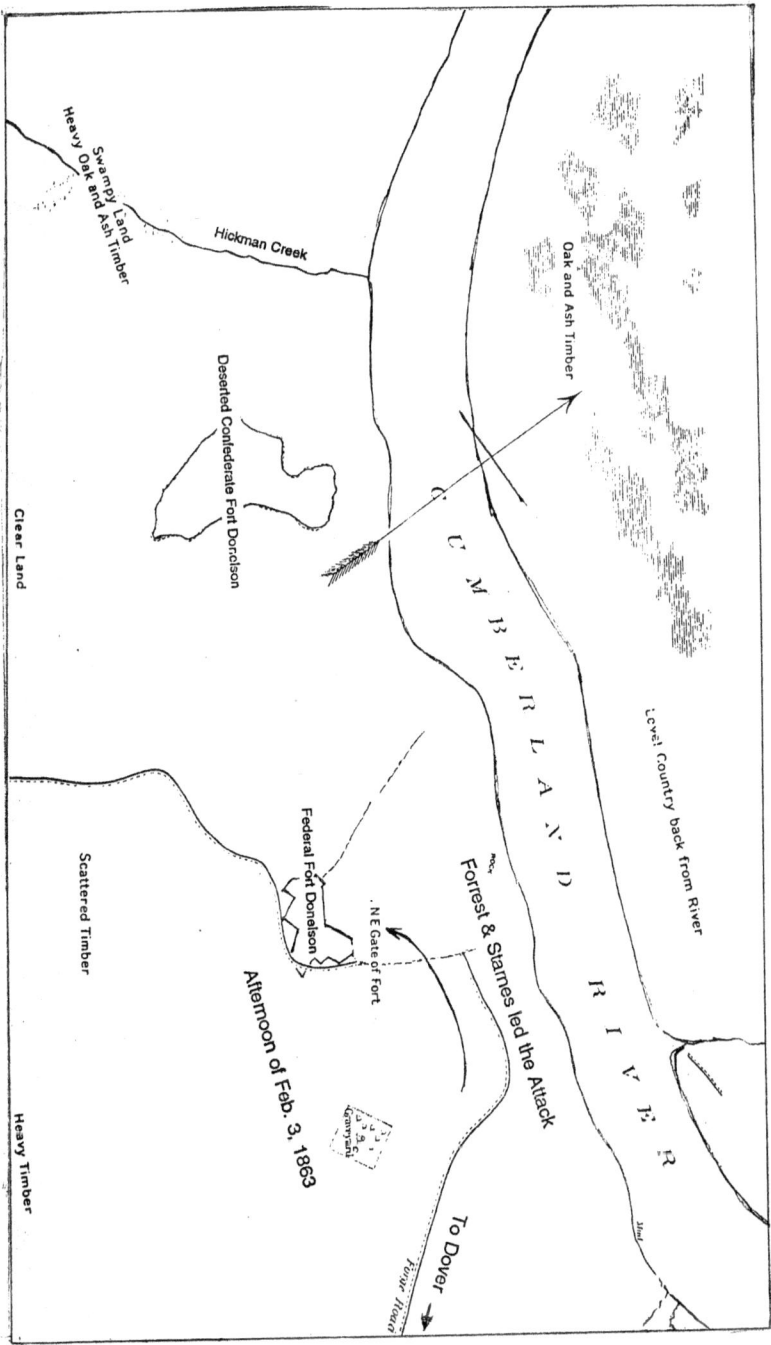

Swampy Land
Heavy Oak and Ash Timber

Hickman Creek

Oak and Ash Timber

Deserted Confederate Fort Donelson

CUMBERLAND RIVER

Level Country back from River

Clear Land

Federal Fort Donelson

N E Gate of Fort

Forrest & Starnes led the Attack

Scattered Timber

Afternoon of Feb. 3, 1863

Cemetery

To Dover

River Road

Heavy Timber

of the town for cover, the cavalry's next advance on foot was made close to the ground. Starnes' men approached the fort from behind the enemy barracks taking every precaution to keep under cover and avoid the casualties of the previous charge as much as possible.

Forrest mounted another horse and led his dismounted men, who drove the Federal sharpshooters out of the houses near the fort and into the fortifications. Col. Starnes realized his company "H" had stopped at the houses in the town, and went back to lead them to the attack. When they came into view about 100 yards from the fort, every cannon and rifle in the fort seemed to volley as one gun. Until the heavy cloud of smoke cleared, Starnes' troopers thought their Colonel and the whole of Company "H" had been blown away and every one of them killed.

Starnes' men said they advanced "right up to the big ditch filled with water. We laid so close to the ground that some of us got away unhurt, but we were in a bad way." Company "F" left two more men dead within a few feet of the fort. His comrades were able to crawl over to Pvt. William P. Rucker, "one of the best men and as fine a soldier as ever shouldered a gun," and bring out his "army letter" and the contents of his pockets to send to his family.

Forrest's horse was again shot from under him and he was badly shaken up in the fall. Every field officer in Starnes' regiment was wounded. Losses were so heavy among the 4th's officers that Maj. C.W. Anderson, of Forrest's staff, said that he had been ordered to command a detachment from that regiment and had led it in the last charge. As the Confederates under Wheeler withdrew from a second costly charge, a conference was called. It was decided that there was not enough ammunition in the whole command to support another charge.

The defeated Confederates went into camp in the deep snow about four miles from Dover "and spent a miserable night." Federal reinforcements from Fort Henry, under Col. W.W. Lowe, made no attempt to follow the Rebels, but five gun-boats, coming to help the beleaguered fort, sent a noisy scream of shells into the cold, snow-covered hills.

Forrest's Brigade took about 200 casualties in killed, wounded and captured. Starnes' losses grieved him greatly, to the extent that he expressed his discomfort with the decision to attack the fort to the men by saying during the battle, "This is Gen. Wheeler's fight." Col. Lowe reported that 135 Rebel dead had been found, and that they then had 50 prisoners. Col. Abner C. Harding, commanding the fort, reported Union losses as 13 killed, 51 wounded and 46 taken prisoners.

On the morning of February 4th the march began back to Columbia, Tennessee. A wide detour had to be taken to the west, by crossing the Duck

River at Centerville, to avoid the column of Federal cavalry and infantry under Brig. Gen. Jefferson C. Davis from Franklin, Tennessee, Starnes' hometown.

Davis had not been punished for the killing of Gen. William "Bull" Nelson in Kentucky. Not only had he been returned to active duty, he had been given command of a division. At the time when he was attempting to cut off Forrest's cavalry, he was commanding the 1st Division, XX Corps, Army of the Cumberland. Having been severely hurt at Fort Donelson and almost out of ammunition, the Confederates dared not risk an encounter with Davis' command. Starnes' regiment of troopers, somewhat demoralized by the lingering thoughts of their brave comrades and friends left lying in the snow in front of Fort Donelson, finally reached Columbia on February 17th.

Pvt. W.H. Whittsitt described the Fort Donelson attack as a "bloody slaughter, in which our regiment suffered greatly... The weather was intensely cold, and the enemy admirably entrenched."

In a few days the regiment moved to Spring Hill and a fine, new camping place east of Thompson's Station, near where the Banks family lived and "where there was plenty of good water." Col. Starnes stayed in this encampment about two weeks, scouting and recruiting in the direction of College Grove and Triune, near his own plantation. Starnes' men said he did everything he could to revive their fighting spirit and confidence, and "to make his regiment as good or better than it ever had been."

About this time an almost eleven-year-old black boy appeared in Forrest's Brigade encampment looking for "Marse Temple." He said that he "hadn't run off, he had kinda slipped off" from Spring Hill, where he was born on the plantation of Captain Absolom Thompson, who had fought in the Indian wars. His name was Marshall and his "Mistis Mickey," Mickey Winn Thompson, had forbidden the young slave boy from running off to join any one of her and the Captain's three sons in Confederate service, Thomas, Dr. J.T.S. and Elijah. Therefore, he had set out to find her nephew in the service, "Marse Temple."

Marshall had been told that his "Marse Temple" was in Morton's Battery of Forrest's Brigade. When the sentries took the boy to artillerist, Charles Temple, he was not the "Marse Temple" Marshall was seeking. The artilleryman told Marshall that his "Marse Temple O. Harris, Jr." was in the infantry (Company "A," 1st Tennessee Inf.). Col. Starnes came along at that moment and Marshall said, "He looked at me kinda laughing and said, 'Looks like a pretty good nigger. Guess he can just come along with me.' And I stayed with him - until they got him." Marshall Thompson became very proud to be Col. Starnes' "personal valet," as he termed his position in the regiment. Even when he complained about the Colonel's passion for high tones in the polish on his cavalry boots, he was proud; "Kept me pretty busy shinning them boots after Colonel rode though high creeks all day."

Marshall Thompson, left (Col. Starnes' Valet) with Louis Nelson

Thompson's Station and Brentwood

In February Maj. Gen. Earl Van Dorn was transferred up from Mississippi, with most of Pemberton's cavalry, and assumed command in Tennessee on the left wing of Bragg's army. His 1st Cavalry Corps consisted of the five brigades of Generals Forrest, Armstrong, Cosby, Martin and Colonel Whitfield, about 6,000 effective horsemen. Forrest, now seeing his brigade as part of a large army, began to understand the value of drilling, military formation and parade reviews. Brig. Gen. Frank Armstrong, who fought as a captain in the U.S. Army at the "First Manassas," had to show him what to do when reviewing his troops. Forrest was so pleased that he ordered two reviews a week for his command.

Responding to Maj. Gen. William S. Rosecrans' order to find out the disposition and intent of these five brigades under Van Dorn, a Federal force of 600 cavalry, 2250 infantry, and artillery with six long-range, rifled Rodman cannon under Col. John Coburn (3rd Brigade, 1st Division, Reserve Corps) set out on a reconnaissance in force from Franklin south toward Spring Hill, Tennessee. Four miles out they collided with Brig. Gen. William H. "Red" Jackson's Division of Confederate cavalry. When Jackson saw the stretched-out Union column, he overestimated their strength and did not feel his forces were strong enough to make an attack. After a two-hour, long-range artillery duel, the Confederates withdrew to Spring Hill and asked Van Dorn for help.

Early on the morning of March 5th Van Dorn positioned his superior force near Thompson's Station on the Alabama & Tennessee Railroad and waited for the Federals to attack. Armstrong's and Whitfield's brigades were on either side of the Columbia Turnpike. Forrest's brigade, and Freeman's Battery of six guns, was on the east end of the Confederate line of battle.

Col. Starnes moved toward the station on the Thompson's Station Road. He halted the regiment and ordered a dismount; the horses were sent back with the horse holders. Forty rounds of ammunition were passed out to each man, and everyone of them knew, "Everything looked like fighting." Starnes rode down the line and marched his men almost to the Columbia Turnpike. The men noted that Forrest's were the only troops west of the pike.

Col. Coburn came up slowly and cautiously, determined to do his duty as best he could. Four of his infantry regiments, with five pieces of artillery, formed a line of advance. On the left of this line, several companies of dismounted cavalry took up a strong position in a dense grove of cedars atop a knoll. Coburn advanced his cavalry demonstration from behind this knoll under Col. Thomas J. Jordan with the objective of taking King's Battery of Whitfield's brigade, which was in a commanding position on the immediate front, and firing rapidly, as were all the artilleries of both sides. Whitfield's brigade and a regiment of Armstrong's were behind a stone wall in a protected position.

Starnes' men could hear the heavy fighting going on about 400 yards northeast of the railroad station and were surprised that their Confederate line on the left was being pushed back to a rock fence on the road from the Columbia Turnpike to the station. There they held. Gen. Forrest came along in a great hurry and gave his orders in a loud voice. "Col. Starnes, the Yankees are on that hill, move up at once and drive them off," he said. With Col. J.H. Edmondson's regiment from the left of Forrest's line, Starnes quickly took the "cedar hill," then pursued the dismounted Union cavalry across the turnpike and onto the railroad. This engagement lasted about an hour, and occurred in conjunction with Whitfield's advance from behind the stone wall on the station road.

Starnes then formed his men in the railroad cut for attack. Gen. Forrest said that the main force of the enemy was on the hill in front of Thompson's Station, across the pike. Meanwhile, Forrest had advanced Capt. Freeman's guns forward to an advantageous position and opened a flanking fire into the Federal line. The Yankee cavalry and artillery had had enough and fled the field in the direction of Franklin. Whitfield's brigade, with Col. S. G. Earle's 3rd Arkansas Cavalry from Armstrong's brigade, charged up the hill and were driven back. Armstrong's entire brigade joined them for the next charge, and again the Rebels failed to drive the defenders from "Coburn's Hill." Armstrong's brigade was badly handled in this affair and lost their battle flag to the 19th Infantry Regiment of Michiganders.

Gen. Forrest reported that the enemy had several times driven back the forces under Generals Armstrong and Whitfield, and his two regiments under Colonels Starnes and Edmondson. Forrest had brought up Col. Jacob Biffle's regiment and Cox's regiment under Lt. Col. Trezevant, and now attacked Coburn's left flank and got to his rear. Col. Starnes charged the hill and drove back the Yankee infantry, who retreated past the Dr. Laws house. As Capt. J.R. Dysart, commanding Company "D," came around the corner of the house to an elevated position on some uneven ground, he was shot through the head and fell over upon Pvt. Whittsitt "with a severe crash." For an instant Whittsitt thought he, himself, had been killed. Pvt. Will Allen was also killed near the Laws house.

One man from each company was sent back about a half mile to the ammunition wagons that had been placed in a low spot on the Columbia Turnpike. The ammunition was brought up quickly. Col. Starnes spoke to his men. "Boys," he said, " the Yankees have got to be driven off that hill; will you do it?" Their response was a resounding "rebel yell" that was referred to as the "infernal screeching of the Rebels" by Col. William L. Utley, 22nd Wisconsin Infantry. While the ammunition was being distributed, King's Battery came up the pike as fast as the horses could run and turned into the Laws' front lot. They began firing over the heads of Starnes' men who were forming their battle line for a charge. The 4th Mississippi Cavalry was in the railroad cut, and Col. Starnes invited their commanding officer to join his 4th

Tennessee in the charge, which he refused. "They seemed to have enough and declined to help us." Col. Starnes notified Capt. King that he was ready to charge the hill and to please cease firing; "...the battle of Thompson's Station was one of the hardest fought."

The charge up Coburn's Hill drove the Yankees westward to the top of the hill, where they turned north toward Franklin, nine miles away. Col. Coburn kept his brigade in compact order as he withdrew. During the attack on his left, Whitfield and Starnes renewed the attack on the right.

In the execution of his retreat, Col. Coburn said he encountered Forrest's Division, which had gained his rear and attacked. Seeing Coburn's men forming for an attack, Forrest ordered Col. Biffle, Lt. Col. Trezevant (commanding Cox's regiment), and Capt. Montgomery Little (commanding Forrest's escort company) to charge. Trezevant was mortally wounded and Little was killed when Coburn's infantry opened fire. When Forrest's 560 charging, dismounted horsemen, who weren't holding horses, were within almost twenty feet of the enemy's line, Col. Coburn ordered a surrender, and his men immediately threw down their arms. One of Starnes' men said their regiment drove Col. Coburn's brigade back, "and good fighters they were, until they met Gen. Forrest with the balance of the brigade and surrendered."

In reporting the engagement and his surrender, Col. Coburn stated that he found they had been opposing Van Dorn's army of six brigades under Generals Forrest, Martin, Cosby, Starnes, W.H. Jackson and Armstrong, and Col. Whitfield. He greatly overestimated their strength at 15,000 men. Beyond the deaths of Capt. Dysart and Pvt. Allen, Starnes' casualties also numbered twenty wounded in the struggle with Col. Coburn.

Col. Starnes' younger brother, Pvt. Samuel Scott Starnes, Jr., was serving in Company "I" of Col. J.G. Ballantine's Mississippi Cavalry regiment in Brig. Gen. George B. Cosby's brigade of Brig. Gen. William T. Martin's Division. On orders of Gen. Van Dorn, Ballantine's regiment was held in reserve to support the Texas Brigade (Whitfield's) during the five to six hours of heavy fighting. The Starnes' had close relatives living in Mississippi. After the occupation of Nashville and the surrounding area, some of the family, who could, left the state to reside with them (as did many other refugees from Middle Tennessee).

Federal losses were 88 killed, 206 wounded and, with the numbers captured, totalled altogether about 1500. The charging Rebel cavalry suffered 357 killed and wounded.

Van Dorn withdrew his forces south to Spring Hill on the evening of March 5, 1863, taking the captured equipment and prisoners with him. Starnes was left with one of Armstrong's regiments to form a strong picket line just south of Franklin. Here he was only about ten miles from his home and the other Starnes family plantations, which had been developed by his late father and his still-living, elderly uncle, John H. Starnes, who was well known in Williamson County for having acquired a measure of wealth and for his thrifty ways. Contrary to the prevailing, early, secessionist, patriotic enthusiasm, the old mill owner and planter invested some of his wealth in gold rather than in Confederate notes and bonds, or in borrowing instruments issued by any one of the seceding states. Pvt. John D. Starnes, who grew up under the care of his older sister and the guardianship of his eldest sibling, Dr. James W. Starnes, enlisted in the cavalry company his physician brother had formed in 1861, and drilled in McGavock's Grove in Franklin.

At this time Brig. Gen. Phillip H. Sheridan was at Eagleville in command of a Union cavalry division. Col. Robert H.G. Minty, 4th Michigan Cavalry, commanding a brigade, notified him that Starnes and Roddy were reported to be on the Chapel Hill Road within a short march of their encampment.

Col. Starnes was very busy at his old camp near Thompson's Station for the next few days looking after the needs of his regiment, maintaining a strong, vigilant picket and scouting the enemy strength and position for intelligence information. Every night he sent twenty picked men into the Union lines to seek any knowledge of enemy plans or anticipated movement. Every morning he had a file of Nashville newspapers to scan. He then moved his camp to Maj. Nathaniel F. Cheairs' (who carried the surrender flag at Fort Donelson) woodlot, but kept his pickets north of Thompson's Station.

The pickets on the Columbia and Lewisburg Pikes were reinforced to at least a full company at each post. On March 8th, Lt. S.S Hughes was in command of "F" Company stationed at Bowden's tollgate on the Columbia Turnpike, about seven miles from Franklin. This was a reserve post with a sergeant's detail advanced to a frontal picket position. Col. Starnes rode up to the post that Sunday morning and was very insistent about alertness and their keeping him informed of the situation on the front. He said, "Boys, don't go back on me. I'm looking for something to happen." The sergeant was then riding out about the James P. Johnson place, keeping someone always watching the pike where it came over Winstead Hill.

About 3 PM a heavy rain began falling, and shortly thereafter the sergeant reported a large body of Union cavalry coming over Winstead Hill. Lt. Hughes relayed the information to Col. Starnes, who replied, "Do your best. Help is coming." The advance picket detail of about twenty men put up a good delaying fight and were not forced back on the tollgate post until sundown. Company "F" used their Enfield rifles to good effect in holding at bay the advancing 2nd Michigan, 9th Pennsylvania and 7th Kentucky until it was near dark, then fell back just south of Ross Alexander's place. They were becoming quite concerned as darkness fell and still no help had arrived.

"Rippa Villa," home of Maj. Nathaniel Cheairs near Spring Hill, TN, where Starnes' regiment encamped in the woodlot in early March 1863

(Five Confederate Generals, Adams, Carter, Gist, Granbury and Stahl, had their last breakfast here before being killed or mortally wounded the late afternoon of November 30, 1864 in the Battle of Franklin)

(A highly emotional confrontation occurred at that breakfast between Gen. Hood and his subordinate Generals over the responsibility for Union Gen. Schofield's forces getting past Hood's army during the night, and into their strong fortifications in Franklin)

(Mrs. Cheairs later related that she was much afraid that they would kill each other in her dining room)

(Maj. Cheairs had been ordered to carry the surrender flag at Fort Donelson on Feb. 16, 1862)

Within an hour, Col. Starnes rode up with his 4th cavalry regiment. Company "F" was on the pike, and the others fell in on both sides of them to form a strong skirmish line for the night, just north of the Alexander place. The Federals went into camp at the old Bowden place and built up huge, bright fires in the evening's damp darkness. Starnes ordered his men to keep quiet and to build no fires. He rode up to the picket line and sent T.M. Andrews and T.R. Tulloss, who was a relative of the Colonel, into the Yankee line to see if they could learn anything. In five minutes Andrews was captured, but Tulloss succeeded in slipping through the enemy pickets. Tulloss said that after getting past the pickets, "everything else was easy." Col. Starnes had heard the capture of Andrews and was surprised when Tulloss came back. Tulloss reported that he had heard the Yankees say that these cavalrymen were the advance of two brigades of cavalry and infantry in a column of 4,000 or 5,000 men. Starnes was not surprised by the information and said that from recent scouting reports, he had expected this enemy movement. He also said that Gen. Phillip Sheridan was in command.

Col. Starnes stayed on the skirmish line most of the night. Everything was very quiet except for one alarm, which fully alarmed Starnes and his men. One shot was fired on the left of their line near the railroad. They thought the Yankees had gone around their skirmish line. One of the troopers on the picket line heard something coming up on his front and ordered a halt. There was no notice taken of the order, so he fired. Upon examination of the body he had brought down, it was found he had killed one of Mr. Ross Alexander's prize-winning jackasses. This was no small embarrassment, since Col. Starnes, the man firing the shot, and several others in Company "F" were from that area and were personally acquainted with Mr. Alexander.

As soon as it was light the Federals advanced on foot and soon drove Starnes' men back. But they retreated in good order and repulsed every attack made upon them. Just north of Spring Hill, Col. Starnes posted Maj. McLemore with a detachment and orders to charge as soon as the Federals came up. Mc Lemore's line was formed a little north of John Wade's house on the east side of the pike, facing the direction of the advancing enemy. Soon the Union cavalry came up riding in fours. McLemore attacked so vigorously that they forced the enemy back up the road north of Thomas B. Bond's place. This action gave Starnes a little time to get his main force though the Spring Hill settlement without a fight.

On a hill south of Spring Hill, two of Freeman's guns were posted and opened fire on the Yankees, which repulsed their advance for awhile. Starnes kept his men well in hand, and with characteristic stubbornness, skirmished with these two brigades of Sheridan's cavalry division, under Col. Robert G. Minty and Brig. Gen. Green Clay Smith, until darkness fell. Late that night he led his troopers across Rutherford Creek on a rickety, old, wooden bridge. When the hindmost rider had cleared the bridge, the Colonel ordered it burned.

Gen. Forrest was waiting on the opposite side of Rutherford Creek with his brigade, ready to dispute any crossing Sheridan's cavalry might attempt. The creek was quite high.

Early the next morning, the Federals moved up to Rutherford Creek. Generals Granger and Sheridan came up and ordered a crossing. Gen. Forrest appeared on the other side with about 500 men. A hot skirmish developed for awhile; Col. Minty and Gen. Smith crossed the creek and Forrest withdrew toward Columbia. Late in the evening of the 10th, Starnes moved his command hurriedly in that direction. When Starnes and Forrest got to the Duck River, they found that the pontoon bridge, over which Van Dorn's army had crossed in retiring from the battle at Thompson's Station, had been carried away by the stream, which was at a very high level of flood stage. They turned left on the Rally Hill Road and rode all night, twenty-five miles eastward (upstream), to cross on White's Bridge and avoid entrapment north of the river. From there they rode to Columbia.

Col. Minty and Gen. Smith followed a mile and a half or two miles toward Columbia, then turned back and recrossed Rutherford Creek. On the 11th the Federal cavalry was back in Franklin. The pontoons were found and placed back in position. By the 15th, Starnes and Forrest were back in their old quarters at Spring Hill. Forrest was made a division commander and Starnes assumed command of the old Forrest's Brigade of cavalry. Forrest's Division was composed of the 1st (Armstrong's) and the 2nd (Starnes') brigades.

The newly-formed, small division was assigned to independent outpost duty on a line that ran roughly from Thompson's Station to the vicinity of College Grove. Starnes was very pleased to be promoted to a brigadier command and to be assigned to duty in the very community in which he had grown up, married, lived, and practiced medicine. On March 21st, he signed a requisition for forage for his five courier horses as Acting Brigadier General.

Col. Starnes had a flock of trusted scouts and informants who reported the deployment and strength of troops in the Franklin and Nashville areas on a daily basis. Upon learning that about 800 troops from the 22nd Wisconsin and 19th Michigan Infantry regiments, that had escaped from the fight at Thompson's Station, were in two, somewhat isolated, garrison positions in Brentwood, Forrest proposed an attack upon them. In a surprise attack, it would be possible to capture this post, halfway between Franklin and Nashville, and bring them away before reinforcements could be brought to their rescue. Gen. Van Dorn approved Forrest's plan, but there were several items of concern that had to be addressed to accomplish this objective.

There was a force of 521 Wisconsin infantrymen, at the fork of the Wilson and Franklin pikes, in a fortification that commanded the approach to the stores and supplies at the Brentwood   station on the Tennessee & Alabama Railroad.   Trees had been felled in all directions for a quarter mile to prevent any surprise advance on the place and enable the garrison to cover any approach with rifle fire.   There were also 230 Michiganders posted in a stockade at the railroad bridge across the Little Harpeth River, only one mile and a half from the encampment.

As ordered, Starnes moved out the night of March 24, 1863 with Biffle's regiment, his 4th Tennessee under Maj. McLemore and a part of Col. James Edmondson's regiment, and crossed the Big Harpeth River at Davis' Mill around midnight, about three miles below his Uncle John H. Starnes' mill. There was a Federal courier line from Franklin to Triune which was directly on his line of march.   Three squads of five men each were detailed to capture the couriers and were told exactly where to find them sleeping.   Unfortunately an inspecting officer had ridden out from Franklin that very day and ordered the couriers to sleep near their houses.   When these men reached the courier posts, they could not find the couriers.   The couriers at Post #1, the Dr. Dan German place, got away on their horses without having been seen, galloped into Franklin and alarmed Gen. Granger.   At Post #2, the Dr. John Crockett home, the couriers' horses were found bridled and saddled in a barn.   Sgt. Tulloss led the horses out, and just as he cleared the building, the couriers opened fire on him from the barn loft, wounding him in the right leg.   His squad was in the barn and they opened up a fire on the Yankees in the loft, making it so hot for them that they ran away in the direction of Nolensville. Post #3, the G.W. Pollard place, was in a strong, log barn, the doors of which were securely fastened, and the attack had to be abandoned.

The Colonel led his men in a northeastward movement, passing within two or three miles of his old home and onto the Wilson Pike.   By 3 AM they had approached Brentwood, cut the telegraph wires to Franklin and destroyed the railroad track near Mallory Station.   He then posted a strong picket on the Franklin Pike at Holly-Tree Gap and approached the Federal garrison from the east about daybreak.   Six companies under Capt. P.H. McBride, Company "I," 4th Tennessee, were ordered to take position just over the top of a hill about 350 yards from the fortified camp.   Edmondson's men were sent to protect the rear against any surprise arrival of Union forces. Everything was now in readiness for the assault, when Gen. Forrest arrived with Armstrong's Brigade.

Daylight came that Wednesday morning, March 25th, and still there was no sign of Forrest and Armstrong.   Since he was without artillery, Starnes reasoned that he was not strong enough to attack the garrison alone and that some unforeseen difficulty must have delayed the planned arrival of Forrest's column from the west. About 7:30 AM, he rapidly moved his command westward toward the Hillsborough Pike, the route by which Armstrong and Forrest were expected.   It was learned that a Federal body of troops was in the vicinity.   Starnes pursued them, only to find it was a firewood gathering detail of nine Negroes who ran away like the devil himself had arrived on horseback, according to a Federal report.

Armstrong and Forrest had encountered some delaying problems in getting a two-gun section of Freeman's Battery across the Big Harpeth some few miles downstream of Franklin. Upon arriving at the designated position and finding Starnes had departed, Forrest, undaunted, prepared to attack without him. Lt. Col. E. Bloodgood, commanding the garrison, who had fled the battle at Thompson's Station, had been rudely awakened earlier in the morning by Starnes' arrival. Bloodgood had then busied his men in loading his wagons and hitching up their teams, in the hope of possibly escaping to Nashville. He first refused Forrest's demand for surrender and made an attempt to make a run for it before the cordon of Rebel forces could be closed around him. Forrest's escort company attacked the head of the column, and they turned back into the camp fortifications. Seeing himself surrounded, with no hope of aid from any other Union force and Forrest's two guns advanced almost to within his works, Lt. Col. Bloodgood surrendered.

Forrest took his escort company, the 4th Mississippi and the 10th Tennessee, and rode hurriedly to the stockade at the railroad bridge. One of Freeman's two guns fired a round. Maj. Anderson, of Forrest's staff, rode in with his dirty, white shirt on a stick, since no one had a white handkerchief, and the 230 men in the garrison surrendered. Both Union fortifications had now been captured without the loss of a single man.

When the couriers who had escaped from Post #1 when Starnes' detail attacked the place about 3 AM, came into Franklin at a gallop, Maj. Gen. Gordon Granger immediately tried to telegraph Lt. Col. Bloodgood to warn him of the impending Confederate attack. But Starnes had cut the telegraph wires. Gen. Granger then quickly dispatched a brigade of Federal cavalry, under Brig. Gen. G.C. Smith, to save Brentwood. After Forrest's capture of the two garrisons at Brentwood, all the supplies and wagons that could not be brought off were burned, as was the railroad bridge. The Rebel cavalry formed a column with the captured wagons and prisoners under guard, and moved hurriedly toward the Hillsborough Pike. The 10th Tennessee was in the rear. A dozen or so stragglers from one of Armstrong's regiments, looking for something to eat, lingered too long at a burning storehouse in Brentwood. They were leisurely following the rear guard when Gen. Smith's 2nd Michigan and 6th Kentucky cavalry regiments galloped down upon them in columns of four with drawn sabers.

These stragglers stampeded into the rear of the 10th Tennessee, commanded by Maj. Wm. E. DeMoss, without any warning whatsoever, and stampeded them. Col. James Gordon temporarily checked the Federal advance with three companies of the 4th Mississippi, who preceded the 10th Tennessee. They were flanked by the 7th Pennsylvania Cavalry and also sent into a wild retreat, since they had volleyed and were holding empty rifles.

Forrest, at the head of the column, came rushing to the rear with his escort and ordered the panic-stricken troopers to halt and form a line of battle. When some of them paid no heed, he grabbed a double-barreled shotgun and fired both barrels into a squad who refused to halt. This action was successful in rallying a fair number of the troops into making a respectable stand.

When he arrived at the Hillsborough Pike, Starnes found that Forrest and Armstrong had already passed to the north and moved eastward toward Brentwood. He turned his command around and hurried back in the direction from whence he had come. He learned from a courier that Forrest had made the captures without him, that a Federal cavalry brigade had followed the column as it moved out to return to Spring Hill, and that there was fighting. Just as Forrest rallied his men, Starnes came up on the Federal flank of Gen. Smith, who had mistaken Gen. Forrest for Col. Starnes and Starnes for Forrest.

Gen. Smith's report:

> The enemy were overtaken about 3 and 1/2 miles from Brentwood, when a running fire was begun and kept up, the rebels falling back for 2 1/2 miles. We recaptured all the wagons and mules, about four hundred stand of arms, a large number of knapsacks, and two loads of ammunition, with one hundred stand of arms dropped by the rebels. Six miles from Brentwood, where several roads come together and cross the Little Harpeth, Colonel Starnes succeeded in bringing the larger portion of his command to a stand, but in ten or fifteen minutes they were driven back giving us command of the crossroads and a strong position.

> At this point a general engagement followed, lasting about one and a half hours. They were again driven back from the woods, ravines and brush. the men were exhilarated with hope and success, and pushed forward in gallant style, when Wharton, with 1,500 cavalry and mounted infantry, appeared close on the right, [Neither Brig. Gen. John A. Wharton nor any of his troops were involved at Brentwood] and General Forrest with a large command on the left. These reinforcements gave Colonel Starnes new courage, and his men rallied on my front.

Col. Starnes' report:

> I moved the force I had with me rapidly on the enemy's right, and charged them with considerable vigor, which caused them to fall back to their position on the hill with great precipitation. They soon rallied, and commenced to deploy for another attack, and I dismounted Col. Biffle's regiment

and part of the 4th Tennessee regiment and moved on them; but finding they were falling back too rapidly to be followed on foot, I made a flank movement on their right wing with three companies under Capt. Allison, pouring a heavy fire into their right and rear. They were retreating very rapidly when General Forrest ordered us to return.

A short time after Starnes had attacked and deployed his two regiments, Forrest came storming up the pike with a medley of several hundred men he had gathered up from various companies and squads. He was cursing loudly and waving a flag, yelling "Fall in every god damned one of you!" Sgt. J.G. Witherspoon and his squad from Biffle's regiment of Starnes' brigade had taken position behind some rocks and trees across a creek from the Union cavalrymen posted behind a stone wall. It was obvious to the sergeant that Gen. Forrest thought he and his men were some of those who had been stampeded, so he fell in quickly at the rear and prepared to charge with the "old man." Forrest dismounted this motley command and threw them into the right flank of Gen. Smith's Yankees, who quickly gave way and retreated two miles toward the railroad. In this counter-attack, they retook all of the wagons Smith had recaptured, but were unable to bring most of them off. The some 800 prisoners, the wagons, mules and horses were marched off to Columbia while Starnes and Forrest moved back to Spring Hill.

The next day, March 26th, Brig. Gen. James B. Steedman, U.S. Army, commanding the Third Division, Fourteenth Corps at Triune, Tennessee, reported that his cavalry was on the Harpeth during the capture of the garrisons at Brentwood, but that he had known nothing of it until 9 AM. He then went toward the Wilson Pike with 400 cavalry, two regiments of infantry and a section of artillery, but found that the enemy had gone to the right (west) of Franklin, and ordered his troops back to camp. "I intend to go to Starnes' [John H.] Mill tomorrow with 150 wagons, escorted by a brigade, and will probably encounter some of the enemy's cavalry."

The disgraceful spectacle of panicked teamsters whipping their teams as the heavy wagons careened down the narrow roads, while equally terrified veteran Confederate cavalrymen tried to force their mounts around them, was, in a measure, partially forgiven, but nothing anyone wanted to talk about or remember. On March 31st the men, officers and their general received a "special commendation" in a general order issued by Gen. Bragg. Despite this melee of stampeding, running and shooting, the Return of Casualties, C.S. Forces, shows four officers and men killed, sixteen wounded, thirty-nine captured or missing. Of his 4th Tennessee, Starnes mentioned only Sgt. Thomas R. Tulloss and Pvt. William W. Osburn wounded, as casualties in his brigade. Chaplain I. Cogshall had also mistaken Gen. Forrest for Col. Starnes:

Between Nashville and Franklin about 8 AM, Starnes' Brigade and two others surrounded the forces at the railroad bridge and demanded surrender. We surrendered because of our small forces. Everything belonging to us was burned on the spot.

A field in front of the former John H. Starnes plantation home near his mill site on the Harpeth River

Former Starnes/Rudder plantation lands near Starnes Creek on McDaniel Road, Williamson County, TN

No. 32.

Requisition for Forage for Public Horses and Oxen, in the service of _____, for _____ days,
commencing the _____ of _____ 186_, and ending on the _____ of _____ 186_,

Date of requisition.	Number of horses.	Number of mules.	Number of oxen.	Total number of animals.	Number of days.	Number of rations.	Pounds of corn.	Pounds of barley.	Pounds of oats.	Pounds of hay.	Pounds of fodder.	Corn. Pounds of	Barley. Pounds of	Oats. Pounds of	Hay. Pounds of	Fodder. Pounds of	REMARKS.

TOTAL ALLOWANCE.

I certify, on honor, that the above requisition is correct and just; that I have now in service the number of animals for which forage is required and that forage has not been received for any part of the time specified.

Received at _____, on the ___ day of _____ 186_, of _____, Quartermaster, _____ pounds of corn, _____ pounds of barley, _____ pounds of oats, _____ pounds of hay, _____ pounds of fodder, in full of the above requisition.

Requisition for
three days forage
for the Courier of
the Courier of the
2nd Brigade Forsetts
Division of Cavalry.
Acting Brig. Gen.
Starnes Commanding

The Attacks on Franklin and Streight's Raid

From the 26th of March to the 9th of April 1863, Starnes' command was on picket, scout and outpost duty between Spring Hill and Franklin. There was almost constant activity in small affairs between the fronts of the opposing armies for diversion, information or even rustling beef cattle gathered to feed the large Union forces. Strong Confederate cavalry forces and the continued threat of assaults on his outposts tended to frustrate Gen. Granger in Franklin. These movements were intended to cause the Union Army commander, Gen. Rosecrans, some concern for his right flank, should he attack the Confederates under Gen. Bragg around Shelbyville. Gen. Granger's March 31st message to Gen. Rosecrans stated, "Forrest, Starnes and Wharton have gone in the direction of the Cumberland River."

Forrest's cavalry's successes were enjoying the attention of the citizenry and southern press and, in particular, the Chattanooga Rebel's account of the Thompson's Station and Brentwood captures. This popularity of Forrest, his officers and men, did not endear him to the higher command of the Army of the Tennessee, such as West Pointers, Van Dorn and Bragg. Van Dorn accused Forrest of knowing that one of his staff had written the very complimentary articles that had appeared in the *Rebel*, crediting Forrest as the commander most responsible for the defeat of the Federals. Forrest denied any such knowledge in a highly emotional confrontation, and Van Dorn accepted his denial, thus defusing the hostility between the two.

Colonel Starnes attacked the Union pickets at his Uncle John H. Starnes' mill on the Big Harpeth River on April 4, 1863. Col. Josiah Patterson, commanding a cavalry regiment, to Lt. Gen. Leonidas Polk, in Shelbyville April 5th:

> My scouts report that Colonel Starnes captured a party of the enemy at Starnes' Mill yesterday evening, camped there with the enemy in line of battle then retired.

Gen. Granger to Brig. Gen. James A. Garfield, Chief of Staff, Army of the Cumberland, USA, April 5, 1863:

> The rebel cavalry that dashed upon our pickets at Davis' Mill [near Starnes' Mill] this morning was Starnes' Brigade. If I had 5,000 cavalry, I would clean out that establishment.

Gen. Van Dorn wanted to draw off troops from Rosecrans' left wing by an attack on Franklin, which was intended to be a reconnaissance in force. There was no attempt to keep this planned action secret. Everyone seemed to know that April 10th was the date of the Confederate advance on the Union stronghold of twice their numbers. Van Dorn rode with W.H. "Red" Jackson's division on the Columbia Pike. About 10:30 AM they drove in the pickets and began the attack, without vigor, on the town. The effective strength of Van Dorn's two cavalry divisions, Jackson's and Forrest's, with Freeman's Battery of six guns, was about 3,100. Gen. Granger stated that he had 5194 effective infantry, 2728 cavalry, eighteen field and two siege guns. There was also Fort Granger on the top of a forty-foot-high knoll on the north side of the Harpeth, where the two twenty-four-pound siege guns and two rifled, three-inch guns were mounted.

Forrest came up the Lewisburg Pike with Armstrong's brigade and two of Freeman's guns. Two miles back, Col. Starnes rode leisurely in front of Biffle's regiment leading his brigade, followed by Capt. Freeman and his other four guns and the 4th Tennessee under Maj. McLemore. From the sound of the cannon, Col. Starnes knew the action was miles away, and neither he nor Capt. Freeman saw the need to throw out flankers. Their years of living in the area and familiarity with the roads and countryside gave them a false sense of security. Sgt. Tulloss, still recovering from the wound to his leg at the courier station during the Brentwood affair, rode beside Col. Starnes as a messenger. The sergeant said that the 10th Tennessee, under Lt. Col. DeMoss, Col. Cox and 300 of his battalion who were captured at Parker's Crossroads and exchanged, and the 11th Tennessee regiment were in the column of march behind the 4th regiment.

Forrest's and Armstrong's advance had run into the Federal infantry posted on the outskirts of Franklin where the Lewisburg Pike enters the town. The Confederate attack so lacked in vigor that Gen. Granger, just a little after noon, was sure it was only a feint and that the real objective was again the garrison at Brentwood. He then ordered out Brig. Gen. G.C. Smith, with all of his cavalry, to save that place again, only to find, after Smith had departed, that the report of Rebels driving in the garrison's pickets, consisted of three or four Negroes walking up the road.

Jackson had driven a fighting 40th Ohio Infantry into town. Forrest and Armstrong increased the intensity of their attack on their eastern end of the Confederate line and opened with a few rounds from Freeman's two guns into the town. Gen. Granger changed his mind and told all the guns to open on any Rebel target in sight, which they promptly obeyed with a thunderous noise of fire and smoke.

Maj. Gen. David S. Stanley, commanding the cavalry corps under Rosecrans, was sent to Franklin with a division of the best Federal cavalry to reinforce Granger. He had arrived about 10 AM from Murfreesboro, and Granger posted him out about four miles on the Murfreesboro Pike with orders to remain north of the Harpeth River and guard the river crossing at Hughes' Mill. Gen. Stanley heard the heavy firing in Franklin in the early afternoon and decided to send his troopers across the river to strike Armstrong from the rear. Forrest's column had been moving past Douglass' Church for some time, and the rear of Armstrong's brigade had passed the church.

Col. Starnes had ordered up his old Company "F," commanded by Capt. James T. Pierce, to act as guides. He sent them along with Capt. Thomas J. Gray's 13-man escort company up to where the road from Hughes' Ford intersected the pike, about a half mile north of Douglass' Church, to look for any sign of the enemy. The 2nd Brigade's line of march was no more than two and a half miles from the Murfreesboro road, and there was a good ford across the Harpeth River near the Dr. Brice Hughes home.

Gen. Stanley sent one of his brigades up the fork of the road that was the nearest route to Franklin and only a mile from the Lewisburg Pike. Another detachment was sent down the other fork a mile and a half to the pike. The 4th U.S. Cavalry, in advance of this detachment, rode from the ford through Dr. Henderson's property on Five Mile Creek, about half a mile east of Douglass' Church, and formed a line of battle on a slight elevation about a half mile east of the Lewisburg Pike on the flank of Starnes' brigade. It was now about 2:30 PM, as twelve-year-old John H. Henderson climbed to the roof of his father's barn to watch the fight he saw coming.

Maj. McLemore said that, at about the top of Hardeman Hill, he had sent a courier to Col. Starnes and requested permission to load the guns of the men of his regiment; the reply was that it was not necessary. When they reached the top of the next hill, he again sent a message to Starnes advising the brigade commander that he thought he saw Yankees on his right by the Henderson house. The courier came back with a message from Acting Brig. Gen. Starnes: "Tell McLemore not to be scared; they are Armstrong's scouts."

Just as Col. Starnes and his staff rode up to the church, Yankees were seen some three or four hundred yards to the east of the pike. At the same time, Capt. Pierce became heavily engaged on the Hughes' Ford road. Starnes sent two of his staff back south on the pike to bring up the other regiments.   He sent Tulloss back a short distance to Col. Biffle with orders to load his guns and take his regiment down Henpeck Lane, dismount his men under cover of the hill, and move through the field toward the Lewisburg Pike. The two men who had been sent after the other regiments were seen running through the fields west toward the Columbia Pike. Then the Colonel told Tulloss to stick to the pike, no matter what happened, and tell McLemore to bring his men.

Tulloss rode uphill about a quarter of a mile and saw Yankees on the east side of the pike all along the top of Oden Hill. Capt. Sam Freeman was the first to see four companies of the 4th U.S. Cavalry bearing down on the battery of four guns. He immediately ordered a halt and threw his guns into position, but before he could load and fire a single shot, the two lead companies of these regulars were upon him, driving back any of McLemore's nearby cavalry whose arms were not loaded. The captain, his guns and some thirty-six men of the battery were quickly captured. The caissons wheeled around quickly and ran back south right through McLemore's men, scattering them in great confusion. Maj. McLemore was west of the pike near Goose Creek, trying to get his men into position. Bugler, Joe Dozier, whose seventeen-year-old son was also in the regiment, was sounding assembly and helping McLemore rally the men. Capt. Freeman and his men were carried off through Dr. Henderson's woodlot in a southeasterly direction.

Starnes heard the tumult to his rear and immediately formed his old Company"F," which had withdrawn down the pike from the road to the ford. They were with Maj. T.F.P Allison, who had served as lieutenant when the company was formed. Col. Starnes personally led the charge. The Federals on their front gave way, and the company rushed up the hill on the east side of the pike and engaged the enemy troopers in front of Dr. Oden's house. The horse given to Col. Starnes by Col. D.C. Kelly the day before was killed just as Starnes crossed the pike. These Federal cavalrymen also quickly retreated in the direction of the Harpeth River.

Gen. Forrest had given Col. Starnes a gold-mounted saber which had been strapped to the dead horse's saddle. The saber was taken from the saddle, presumably by one of the departing Yankees, and never recovered.

Col. Biffle's 9th Tennessee was coming down a slope about a mile south of Douglass' Church when Sgt. Tulloss arrived with orders from Starnes. When they got to the church, they turned east up Henpeck Lane. Just then they heard rapid firing on the pike near Freeman's battery, which was then across a field from them and south of the church. They went up a hill to a thicket on the side of a bluff near a spring on the south side of the narrow lane. Col. Biffle jumped off his horse and ordered every man to dismount, load his gun and follow him at the double-quick. While they were moving across the bottom toward a rock fence, the enemy opened fire on Biffle's men, kicking up the dirt at their feet but hitting no one. The dismounted troopers returned the fire as they ran toward the battery.

The Federals were in plain view and had captured the battery, with little resistance, before Biffle's Confederates arrived on the scene. Just before the regiment reached the battery, they noticed the Yankees retreating. At the same time, another detachment of the enemy made a movement on Biffle's rear. He ordered half his men to about-face to meet this threat. In executing this movement, Company "F" of the 9th was cut in two. Some of the men in front were so intent upon going after the regulars who had captured the battery, they hadn't heard the command.

When they saw the Yankees retreating rapidly, this portion of the regiment swung to the left, crossed to the east side of the pike and advanced through Henderson's woodlot to cut them off. 2nd Sgt. J.G. Witherspoon, finding no commissioned officers in this group of Company "F," took charge. Noticing a dozen or more Federals lagging behind, between them and the battery, these Rebels made a run for the fence to cut them off.

This lagging group had captured Capt. Sam Freeman. Seeing Biffle's men moving through the woodlot, the regular cavalry ordered their prisoners to "double-quick" at pistol point or they would be shot down. Capt. Freeman replied that he could run no faster, since he was thoroughly exhausted from the effort he had already made and was still making. The battery's Asst. Surgeon, Dr. Skelton, was running with Capt. Freeman. A bullet passed through the doctor's hand as he threw it up asking their captors not to shoot. Capt. Freeman was shot in the mouth, killed by a pistol fired in his face.

The detail that had shot Capt. Freeman and Dr. Skelton went over the woodlot fence less than 100 yards from Sgt. Witherspoon's running squad from the 9th Tennessee. Witherspoon told two of the best shots in his company, Pvts. Joe Duncan and Nat Montague, to kneel down by a tree, take good aim and try to get some of them as they went by on horseback. These men then went past the place where Capt. Freeman lay dead, no more than 100 yards from his battery. Two or three men were with him who had been captured and left behind in the Yankees' haste to get away. One very young man was crying, bitterly cursing the Yankees and swearing vengeance for the "brutal murder." They then marched up to the battery. By that time the balance of Biffle's regiment had already arrived at the battery. In charging up to the battery, several received wounds and one man was killed.

Maj. McLemore had been able to form some of his men and take part in the repulse of the U.S. Cavalry. Bugler Joe Dozier captured three Yankees and killed one, who the boys said, would certainly have killed McLemore.

When Gen. Stanley's advance unexpectedly ran into and surprised Starnes' brigade, two couriers galloped up to Armstrong's front and yelled to General Forrest at the top of their voices, "General Stanley has cut in behind you, attacked Starnes' brigade, captured the battery and is right at Armstrong's rear."

Another facet of Forrest's military genius showed as he realized the excited voices were spreading panic in the ranks. He said, "You say he is in Armstrong's rear, do you? Damn him, that's just where I've been trying to git him all day, I'll be back directly...." He ordered Armstrong to face his line about and push his skirmishers forward, said he was going to Starnes and rode away with his escort company. Armstrong's men thought it just another Forrest trap.

Forrest galloped up with his escort to participate in the last charge, driving the Yankees across Hughes' Ford. He then rode at a gallop to the large, lifeless form of his battery commander on the ground, dismounted, knelt by his side and grasped the still warm, limp hand of Capt. Samuel L. Freeman. Visibly shaken, his voice broke and he could say only, "Brave man; none braver."

Starnes' brigade formed on the recaptured battery. The wheels of the guns had been cut down by the captors. One gun was propped up on the pike with fence rails. Two or three boys from Biffle's Company "C" had also been drilled in artillery firing and they took charge of the gun and fired two or three shots in the direction of a considerable force of troops that had come into view. Someone thought the flag they saw was the familiar Texas emblem, and a courier came dashing down the pike yelling, "Cease firing, cease firing, that is Armstrong's Brigade."

The whole affair had not lasted more than a half hour. 2nd Sgt. J.G. Witherspoon said it seemed to him "that somebody blundered; for if the brigade had had their guns loaded, it wasn't likely that Capt. Freeman would have been captured." Pvt. Martin Houston of Company "C," 9th Tennessee, was at a loss to know why Col. Biffle didn't form his men on horseback on the pike, load their guns and charge the Yankees, "instead of going up that little land on foot. We certainly could have relieved the battery very quickly."

Col. Starnes had been incautious in not having a loaded gun in his brigade and no flankers out in front and to the right of his column of march. With his usual, quick recognition of a perilous situation and instant reaction, he skillfully managed to retake the battery and drive the attacking force back across the river. Forrest later admitted, privately, that when the couriers informed him of Gen. Stanley's attack on Starnes' flank, he thought his whole command was "gone up."

Starnes' men pressed Dr. Henderson's wagon and team to remove Capt. Freeman and their other dead to Spring Hill. The wagon team was driven by a Negro accompanied by young John Henderson, who had quickly come down from the roof of his father's barn, " when the bullets began to whiz by." They arrived in Spring Hill late at night, unloaded the bodies at residences, then spent the night in a tent with the soldiers at their encampment. Shortly after the boy and the Negro had arrived home and put the team of mules in the barn, they saw the Yankees come and take them. Dr. Henderson had not been aware that his son had gone to Spring Hill with the Confederate dead.

Starnes reported his losses as six killed, seventeen wounded and thirty-one captured. Among the seventeen killed in Gen. W.H. Jackson's Division, in the attack on Starnes' hometown of Franklin, was the Colonel's youngest brother, twenty-three-year-old Pvt. Ebenezer Starnes, a courier from Company "A" in the 7th (Duckworth's) Tennessee Cavalry Regiment. Ebenezer was buried inside the walled fence of huge stones surrounding the Starnes family cemetery built by their father, Dr. Samuel Scott Starnes, on the north side of the Harpeth, nine miles east of the town.

Van Dorn's forces fell back to Franklin. The Federal cavalry stayed in Franklin the next day, Saturday, then marched back to Murfreesborough

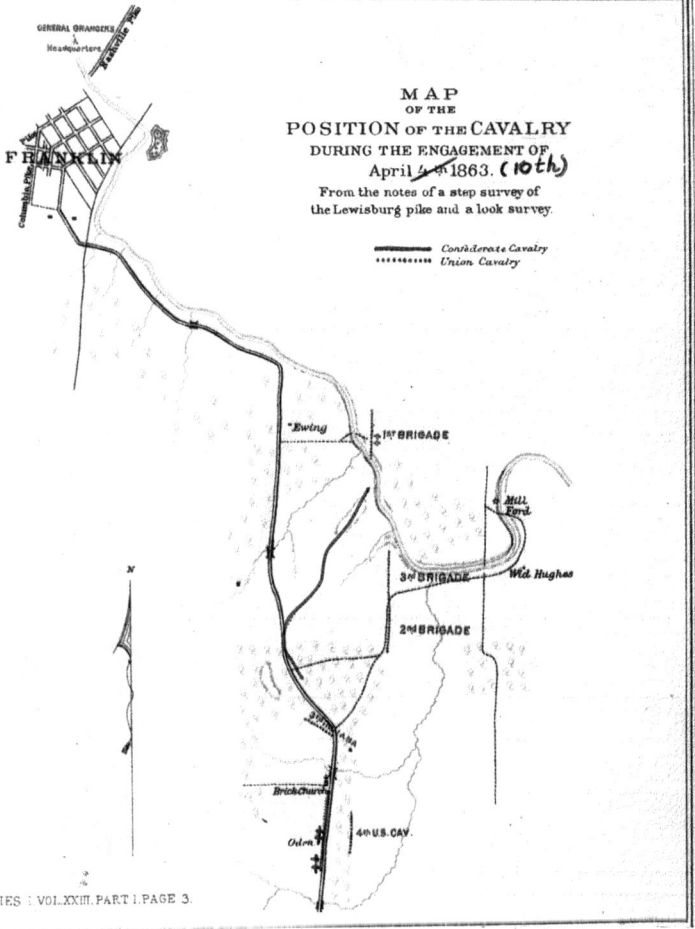

MAP
OF THE
POSITION OF THE CAVALRY
DURING THE ENGAGEMENT OF
April 4th 1863. (10th)
From the notes of a step survey of
the Lewisburg pike and a look survey.

━━━━━ Confederate Cavalry
•••••••••• Union Cavalry

GENERAL GRANGER'S
Headquarters

FRANKLIN

"Ewing
1st BRIGADE

Mill
Ford

3d BRIGADE   M'd Hughes

2nd BRIGADE

BrickChurch

Odem   4th U.S. CAV.

N

**Starnes' Brigade attacked on the Lewisburg Pike; Capt. Freeman
captured and killed**

Massive hued stones mark the Dr. Samuel S. Starnes family cemetery

Tombstone of Pvt. Ebenezer Starnes, killed during Van Dorn's "Reconnaissance in Force" Attack on Franklin, TN, April 10,1863

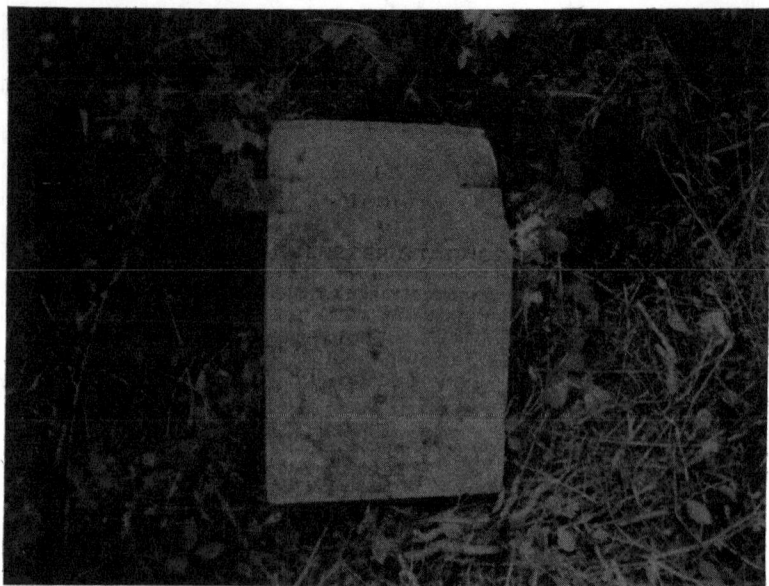

and burned ten dwellings and outhouses belonging to people who had sons in the Confederate Army per the order of a frustrated Gen. Stanley, according to Col. D.M. Ray, 2nd Tennessee (Union) Cavalry, commanding a brigade.

Saturday night, April 11th, the day after the attack, Forrest's Division camped in the woods near Cowles' Schoolhouse, seven miles from Franklin. Col. Starnes sent Sgt. Tom Tulloss to Squire Chapman's, a personal friend of the Colonel's, to spend the night. Another man of "F" Company accompanied the Sergeant, who could not walk without crutches.

On Sunday Pvt. Whittsitt of Starnes' old Company "F" (who, after the war, became well known as Reverend W.H. Whittsitt, D.D) officiated at the funeral of Capt. Samuel Freeman:

> General Forrest stood at the side of the grave, his tall form bent and swayed by his grief. It was a sight to remember always, the sternest soldier in the army bathed in womanly tears and trembling like an aspen with his pain. The whole army sympathized in the mighty sorrow.

Confederate cavalry successes in the Columbia and Franklin area were continuous irritations to Union General Rosecrans following his doubtful victory at Stones River the first of the year. Their scouting and picketing activity kept Union foraging parties close to their lines, and he could not move on Bragg as long the cavalry protected his left flank. Rosecrans believed that more and better horses and horse soldiers would be the solution. He sent a barrage of complaining wires to the annoyance of the authorities in Washington. They sent him boatloads of animals, most of which were young, wild, or otherwise unserviceable as cavalry horses.

Rosecrans claimed the Confederate cavalry outnumbered his cavalry about five to one. The returns show that it was actually about two to one. After this last reconnaissance in force, Gen. Granger tried to tell Rosecrans that he didn't understand why it was so difficult to surprise and crush Van Dorn's cavalry: "He keeps every road and lane and hilltop for miles picketed; the country people are his friends and are always ready to give information." But Gen. Rosecrans was tired of excuses and was receptive to the proposal of Col. Abel D. Streight, 51st Indiana Cavalry, to conduct a raid into north Georgia to cut Confederate lines of communication and cut off the supply of guns, ammunition and supplies which made it possible for the Southerners to carry on the war.

On the afternoon of the cavalry fight on the Lewisburg Pike, Col. Streight received orders to embark on the steamers in Nashville and begin the expedition. This brigade of mounted infantry on eight steamers traveled down the Cumberland and Ohio and up the Tennessee River to rendezvous with the forces of Brig. Gen. Greenville M. Dodge at East Port, Mississippi. Streight's some 1250 mules, 2,000 men and equipment were unloaded on April 19th. The plan was for Gen. Dodge's forces to threaten Tuscumbia, Alabama, while Streight was to stay to his rear to throw the Confederates off his trail. Then, at an opportune time, Streight would break away and make a dash for the mountains.

The only opposing Confederate force in the area was the small cavalry brigade of Col. Phillip D. Roddey. This command succeeded in harassing Gen. Dodge's advance on Tuscumbia. Some of the farm boys in Roddey's command had heard the unmistakable noise of a thousand mules braying when their feet landed on solid ground. They sneaked into Col. Streight's holding enclosures under cover of night. About 400 of the best half-wild, young mules were stampeded into the countryside by the yelling and firing of rifles and pistols. Streight was delayed almost two days, catching about 200 of the critters; the Rebs caught most of the rest of them.

Streight's mounted-infantry, mule brigade filed out from East Port the afternoon of April 21st at the rear of Dodge's force. Dodge's men skirmished with Rebels on their front and didn't reach Tuscumbia until 5 P.M. on the 24th. This delay allowed Gen. Bragg to hear of the situation and order Forrest, on the 23rd, to take his old brigade and move hurriedly from Spring Hill to Roddey's relief, take command and check the Federal advance.

Col. Edmondson's 11th Tennessee was immediately hurried off to cross the Tennessee River at Bainbridge and join Col. Roddey. Col. Starnes had become seriously ill and was taken to the Parkes home on the Hampshire Pike near Columbia. Maj. McLemore led the 4th out with the 9th and 10th Tennessee regiments and the battery, now commanded by Lt. John Morton. They crossed the Tennessee River at Brown's Ferry near Courtland, Alabama on the 26th. Just before crossing, Gen. Forrest ordered Col. Dibrell to take his 8th Tennessee and one gun, follow the north bank of the river toward Florence, Alabama and create a diversion in the Federal rear at every opportunity.

A courier, young Pvt. Samuel P. Claybrooke, stayed behind to care for Col. Starnes during his illness. "Courier Sam" had made quite a reputation for himself at Parker's Crossroads by carrying messages back and forth for Col. Starnes in the heaviest of the firing. And he had repeated this dangerous riding exhibition at all subsequent encounters. Starnes had presented him with a pair of pistols for capturing three Union officers by himself, and complimented him for gallantry at Humboldt and Parker's Cossroads. Claybrooke volunteered to care for the Colonel, but was concerned that this was the only action he had missed since having rejoined Starnes before the skirmish at Readyville. It turned out to be the only fight of the 4th Tennessee Cavalry that Claybrooke missed during the whole war. Lt. Sydney S. Hughes, "F" Company, said that Sam Claybrooke rode straight to the points to which he was sent, even when under dangerous, close fire.

Col. Streight was quite concerned by a message from Gen. Dodge saying there was no doubt that Forrest had crossed the river on the 23rd and reached the vicinity of Town Creek. Even "the wizard of the saddle" could not have moved rapidly enough to be already on Streight's front.

Gen. Dodge had about 5,500 infantry and cavalry, and pushed Roddey across to the east side of Town Creek. Forrest arrived none to soon to save him. "Preacher" Whittsitt said that Gen. Dodge pressed them sorely all day on Monday, the 27th, and also on the 28th. In forming his line of battle on the 28th, Forrest posted Starnes' and Biffle's regiments out of artillery range on the Tuscumbia Pike. A five-hour artillery duel and a full day of skirmishing followed.

After dark, when the fighting had ceased and the Federals had withdrawn across the creek and gone into camp for the night, Mr. James Moon, a citizen from Tuscumbia, arrived in camp with a message for Gen. Forrest. He had ridden through and around several Union detachments to tell Forrest that an estimated 2,000 Federal troops had ridden through Mt. Hope toward Moulton. Streight had left Tuscumbia on the 26th, marching south to Russellville, then turning eastward to Mt. Hope in the rain, mud and darkness, over an almost impossible, rocky road. Gen. Rosecrans had intended that Dodge go no farther than Town Creek. But when informed that Forrest was at Town Creek, Streight insisted that Gen. Dodge should attack and drive the Confederates at least as far as Courtland, or better, to Decatur, Alabama.

Forrest, upon receiving word of Streight's movements, immediately called a staff meeting. Maj. McLemore was ordered to prepare his regiment, as was Col. Biffle, and the artillery ordered to prepare quickly for pursuit. Three days' rations were cooked, and shelled corn for two days forage was issued. Starnes' men said it was then "boots and saddles," and at 1 AM on the 29th, as Col. Streight left Moulton, Forrest started after him. During the forenoon of that Wednesday, they reached Moulton. After an hour or so of rest, they departed the town with a 1200-man "rebel yell" in two divergent columns. The 4th rode in the column heading northeast. They followed the Yankee raiders for seventeen miles in a cold rain over the muddy road, to within four miles of Day's Gap, where they found them encamped. It was, by then, a little after midnight. But it took several hours for all the tired troopers and horses to come in to feed and sleep.

Streight was surprised that Forrest had caught up with him so quickly. He was now well aware of the gross error of using mules as reliable animals for mounting infantrymen because of their supposed toughness, and sure-footedness on the mountains. Also, he was told they could survive on less and poorer forage than could horses. So far, Streight's "lightning mule brigade" was certainly not living up to the expectations of Gen. Rosecrans and the Union planners of the expedition. He had been three and a half days on the march and covered a distance of only sixty-five miles.

"What's the use of mounting his command if they're going to march at the rate of infantry?" one of the 4th's troopers asked. When no mount was available, many a cavalryman could be seen riding a mule as a last resort instead of marching as an infantryman. Any farm boy had observed mules struggling at top speed and still falling behind horses travelling leisurely at the "long lope." Mules, when pushed beyond their own natural speed of traveling, will break down rather soon. This is especially the case when they are ridden as mounts. At daybreak the tired Rebels were awakened by an awful, echoing chorus of over a thousand braying "sons of a jackass."

At 9 AM Forrest prepared to attack Streight in his camp on Sand Mountain. Biffle was sent with his and Starnes' regiments, under McLemore, hurrying through the neighboring passes to take Streight's forces in the flank and rear. From his two companies of Union Alabamians, under Capt. D.D. Smith, Streight knew about these passes and the likelihood that Forrest would utilize them. These men were from the Alabama sand hill country and knew every hill, creek, path and rock in the whole area.

Col. Streight was a very capable officer and knew he had to make a stand and fight. About two miles from the top of the western crest of the mountain, he carefully chose the position for his first ambuscade. The forming of the battle line on a circular ridge had hardly been completed when Smith's Alabamians in the rear guard, who were still lagging around their camp fires, came dashing into the line. Capt. Bill Forrest and his scouts were so close on their heels that they could not stop their horses and turn back before Streight's men, on both sides of the road, poured a volley into the company of scouts, shattering the Captain's thigh bone, killing and wounding several of his men.

Forrest came up at the head of his advance. Edmondson's men were dismounted and posted in the center; Roddey's regiment and Julian's mounted battalion were deployed on the right. The escort, and what was left of the scouts, were placed on the left, barely a thousand Confederates in line for the attack. Morton's two guns were brought up the mountain and opened fire on the Federal line from a range of only about 300 yards. Edmondson's trained men moved steadily to within 100 yards of the enemy lines. The mounted escort and scout companies on the left rode into Streight's skirmishers. Roddey's and Julian's men recklessly pushed their horses ahead of Edmondson's troopers into an advanced, exposed position and brought a murderous volley on themselves from the larger portion of the Union line. A number of horses and men were killed or wounded.

Seeing the confusion in the Rebel advance, Streight ordered a charge. Edmondson and the scout and escort companies fell back in some semblance of order and made an effort to help the artillerists take the two guns away. Several artillery horses had been shot and became entangled in their harnesses. The field pieces and their caissons could not be moved in time and were captured by the Federal advance. Forrest went into a rage and laid the blame on Lt. A. Wills Gould, in command of the guns, for their loss. In his angry ravings he wished he had Starnes and Biffle, but McLemore and Biffle were miles away. The "old man" dismounted everyone and ordered every horse tied to a bush; there was to be no man spared to hold a horse. When they counterattacked, about 11 AM on April 30th, they found only the rear guard, who quickly mounted their mules and rode away.

"They whipped Roddey in the initial encounter in the morning... and captured two of the guns of Morton who commanded after the death of Freeman ," was Pvt. Whittsitt's comment.

Six miles eastward from the morning battle site, where a byroad came into the main road, Forrest was overjoyed to see the 4th and 9th Tennessee riding rapidly in the distance. There had been just too many miles for them to cover in bypassing Day's Gap to get to the rear of the fast-moving Streight, who was aware of their maneuver. The Federals had passed before Biffle's and Starnes' regiments could strike the road in front of them. "Preacher" Whittsitt had a few words to say about Col. Streight's change of pace:

> He had been three and a half days on the march when we struck him and had traversed a distance of only sixty-five miles. He must have considered that he was on a May-Day frolic. After we came up with him, he moved at the rate of fifty miles a day and threw in some fighting besides.

Gen. Forrest ordered Col. Roddey, with his regiment and Julian's battalion, to backtrack and take a position of observation on Gen. Dodge's front. He did not know that Col. Dibrell had carried out his orders so completely to harass Gen. Dodge. After having spread the word that Gen. Van Dorn was on his way to the area, the cautious Dodge withdrew back toward Corinth. Edmondson's regiment, accompanied by Maj. Charles W. Anderson of Forrest's staff, was sent out in the general direction of Somerville and Brooksville to travel a parallel course with Streight and keep between him and the Tennessee River, should he attempt to escape via Guntersville and cross the river.

"Old Forrest" did not know what Streight's plans and intentions were and, therefore, in his usual manner, had to cover all possibilities that he could. Dispatching Roddey, Julian, Edmondson and all the artillery except four guns to distant assignments left him with only the veteran regiments of Starnes' 4th, Biffle's 9th, his escort and his seriously wounded brother, Bill's "Forty Thieves" scout companies to use for pursuit, less than half of Streight's numbers. About nine miles from Day's Gap, the blue of the Federal guards came into the view of the 4th's vedettes. The General had ordered them, "Shoot at anything blue and keep up the scare." A running fight began on the road, continued for a mile and pressed Streight's men so closely that he "was compelled to prepare for battle." The capable Streight chose a strong, defensive position on a ridge called Hog Mountain. The chatter of the pickets' musketry became heavier and heavier as more and more troopers became involved. By an hour before dark, the whole force became engaged. This was future minister, Pvt. W.H. Whittsitt's first night battle and he was much impressed by it:

> The Pine trees were very tall, and the darkness from their shade was very intense, the mountain where the enemy was posted was very steep, and as we charged them again and again under Forrest's own lead it was a grand spectacle. It seemed the fires which blazed from their muskets were almost long enough to reach our faces. There was one advantage of being below them; they often fired above our heads.

Streight's men fought well and were well commanded by their officers. They repulsed every charge for almost three hours. At eight o'clock Col. Jacob Biffle had been ordered to form the few men held in reserve, move by the left flank and attack the mule holders. The escort was sent out to the right on the same mission. After some delay in getting around Streight's flank and into position, Forrest heard the sounds of confusion to the enemy's rear. The mule holders were under attack. The men, who did not know that Col. Roddey had departed and was on his way to Decatur, thought his full force had attacked the enemy flank. They descended on Streight's line with great enthusiasm to find only a light rear guard to chase from the field of battle. The guns captured in the morning fight had been spiked and their carriages cut down, but it was a great moral victory to recover them.

The battle had ended about 10 PM and "shortly after the moon rose in great splendor. It seemed to be sent for our special behoof." The dangerous game of pursuit and avoidance of ambuscade began all over again. Butternut-clad riders buried the recovered guns in the sand. Joe Dozier's bugle, and that of the 9th's bugler, blared assembly and they rode off in the moonlight.

Col. Streight was pursued so closely that he soon thought he'd better give these Tennessee Rebels a check. He remained with the rear guard in person and selected a place about twenty yards off the road to set a trap with Col. Gilbert Hathaway's 73rd Indiana regiment in a dense, pine thicket. Forrest expected it and threw Biffle ahead with a small advance of only a few riders out front. These leading scouts expected death from behind every tree or growth of brush.

Pvt. Granville Pillow, from Capt. Groves' Company of Biffle's command, was one sent forward. His horse was moving along at a good pace when it suddenly stopped, threw up its head, pointed its ears and sniffed the spring night air. Pillow believed in "hoss sense," rode back and reported to his lieutenant, who then sent him to the General. "Old Bedford" believed in good horse sense too. This was what he had hoped for. He sent Pillow and two other volunteers forward until they detected the presence of the enemy or drew his fire. Forrest also had the artillerists of Ferrell's Battery, under Lt. Jones, take their horses out of harness and quietly push a gun down the road, double-shotted with canister. It was then about 11:30 PM.

The advance Rebel threesome appeared to ride carelessly, but were moving cautiously and watching for the slightest sound or movement. Dark figures rose in the pine thicket, and flashes from the muzzles of Col. Hathaway's Indianian's guns sent the three horsemen flying back, lying as low as they dared over the sides of their mounts. Pillow brought Gen. Forrest forward and showed him where the Indiana troops were posted, and they pointed out the position so the gunners could aim their piece. This pointing and training of a field gun by moonlight was an usual experience for the artillerist. But, on Forrest's signal, he pulled the firing lanyard and the canister tore through the thicket, as small arms fire from the cavalrymen crackled in the night. Another gun was brought up and fired two or three shells down the road. The raiders returned rifle fire, but cannon shell and canister fire were not what was expected by Streight's ambushing troopers. They quickly remounted their mules and were off again. A line of torn, paper scraps from destroyed personal papers was found all along the line on which the Yankees had formed. This told the Rebels, "It was clear that their alarm had become serious and would help us much if we could keep it up."

Six miles further, between 2 and 3 AM in the morning when most of the command was dozing in their saddles, Streight again set up another ambush. A small detachment lay in the undergrowth at the foot of a steep causeway on which the Rebels were marching to a ford on a branch or tributary of the Black Warrior River. Streight's opening fire caused some initial confusion among Forrest's worn-out men and inflicted some losses, particularly among the animals. The detachment was scared; unable to take advantage of the situation, they ran across the stream as soon as they discharged their weapons. Most of the fire came from those drawn up on the opposite side of the river, who also withdrew. After having crossed the river, Gen. Forrest allowed his men to "get down and sleep from 3 to 5 AM," May 1, 1863. All the corn they had was fed to their horses, and the men lay down and slept where they were.

Col. Streight kept his tired men going, winding down the eastern slope of Sand Mountain and into the corn-growing valley. They reached Blountsville about 10 AM and gathered up every horse and mule in the countryside, and all the corn the citizens could supply. This was the first time the people of the town had seen any blue uniforms, and they were treated to a May Day's entertainment.

Streight saw the need for a faster pace and lightened his load by transferring the contents of his wagons to the backs of the pack mules. The ammunition was distributed and rations were issued. The wagons and discarded supplies were then set afire. As the smoke rose from the bunched wagons, Gen. Forrest charged into the village at the head of his escort company and a portion of Starnes' 4th Tennessee. They drove Capt. Smith's rear guard through and out of town in a cloud of dust and into Streight's main column. The Confederates then went back to extinguish the flames and recover some much-needed supplies. One of the men said, "We immediately put his column in motion and kept it on the run [about ten miles] to the Black Warrior where he was compelled to fight us to obtain a crossing."

Under the cover of a heavy skirmish line, Streight got his main body across the rocky ford with the loss of only two pack mules carrying two boxes of hardtack each. Two howitzers on the east bank covered the hectic withdrawal of the skirmish line as the Tennesseeans charged, taking some prisoners. Col. Streight said that the last of his men got across by 5 PM. Forrest detailed two companies of Biffle's regiment to push on and "worry them." A trooper in Starnes' 4th said, "Here we were allowed to rest from 6 PM until the moon rose about eleven." One young trooper retrieved a box of wet hardtack from a dead mule.

During the rest, while the famished critters were eating their corn, Forrest went among them and culled out the weakest animals to be sent back to Decatur. Then he spoke words of thanks and encouragement to the men. About 600 rode out of the camp in pursuit of close to 1700.

Just before daybreak the Rebel command caught up with Biffle, who was skirmishing with the raiders at the Big Wills Creek crossing. Forrest sent him and his two companies to the rear for a needed rest, and the "old man" took over the advance lead with his escorts. Streight rushed his force across the creek without a contest, but in the hurry, some of his powder got wet.

Col. Streight still held a decided advantage over Gen. Forrest. Streight's men had swept the countryside all along the way, impressing every horse and mule they could find for fresh draft and mount animals. Corn cribs were emptied and long, fodder-storage shocks were taken to feed them. Despite their fighting spirit, more and more of Biffle's and McLemore's veterans were dropping behind. Their worn-out horses were throwing shoes, pulling up lame, or suffering from too little grain and too much of the April grasses. When details were sent back, they would find exhausted men sleeping so soundly by the side of the road, that they could not be awakened without some intense effort. The ever vocal Pvt. William H. Whittsitt summed up the situation:

> He [Col. Streight] recruited his horses almost every mile. It was a common thing to find, standing in the highways, the wagons and carriages of the citizens from which he had removed the horses, leaving his exhausted mules in their place. Our horses were falling

out constantly, and we had no means whatever of renewing the supply.

Four miles eastward of Big Wills Creek, Forrest, leading the advance, caught up with Streight at the rude, uncovered, wooden Black Creek Bridge. One of Col. Streight's blue-clad scouts was riding hard in front of the Rebels who were close upon his heels. He was ordered to "halt and surrender." His capture was made by the General himself. Pvt. Whittsitt described his view:

About 11 AM, of May 3rd [2nd] we came in sight of the Black Creek Bridge, and perceived that it was on fire, which indicated that the enemy were all on the other side.

Some two hundred yards from the bridge was the humble home of the Widow Sansom and her two daughters. Her son was away in the 19th Alabama Infantry, C.S.A. The widow and her daughters had rushed out to try to save their fence, which ran up to the bridge, when they saw the smoke. When they reached the bridge, they saw the rails from their fence burning in a pile of wood in the middle of the bridge. They were on their way back to the house when Gen. Forrest rode up, told them who he was, and asked where the Yankees were. The widow said that they were behind a small rise across the creek, and if his men showed their heads above it, "they will kill the last one of you." The skirmishers got into position and opened fire across the creek. Forrest stopped the younger Sansom daughter and asked her where the creek could be crossed.

Seventeen-year-old Emma told him that there was an unsafe bridge two miles away, but that was not what he wanted to hear. She then said that there was an old ford a few hundred yards away that was known only to her family. Their cows used to cross there during dry spells. She rode up behind the General and showed him the place where the stream might be crossed. They crawled up to the ford so the girl could point out where the cows entered, moved to midstream, and went up the bank on the opposite side while the fire of the skirmishers was growing rather heavy.

Troopers held the ammunition on their critters, who were belly deep in the creek, and quickly ferried the contents of the caissons across. Ropes were tied onto the guns, and they were pulled across and up the muddy bank. Col. Streight had anticipated that the burning of the bridge would delay Forrest's advance by at least half a day. In about a half hour the Rebels were on the east side of the creek and had driven off the Federal rear guard.

Streight did not linger in Gadsden, Alabama. He surrounded the town in order to corral all the horses and mules of the local citizenry, burned some houses containing small commissary stores and moved on toward Rome, Georgia. Forrest had come up on his rear and kept up a continuous skirmish until 4 PM, when Streight ordered a halt at Blount's Plantation, twelve miles from Gadsden. While Streight fed his animals, Forrest advanced his sharp-shooters and kept up a show of strength and aggressiveness until dark.

During the half hour Forrest had remained in Gadsden, he obtained the courier services of Col. John H. Wisdom, who was to ride a parallel course on the south side of the Coosa River and advise the city of Rome, Georgia of their peril. From Turkey Town, eight miles east of Gadsden, Streight sent out Capt. Milton Russell, with 200 of his best mounted men, with orders to hurry on to Rome, and seize and hold the bridge until the main column of the command arrived.

Union sharpshooters were scattered in a stand of Oldfield pines, and a barricade was placed in a sharp turn in the road to force the Rebels to cross an open field in any assault. Behind a rise at the end of the field, Col. Hathaway posted five hundred rifles under his able command to complete Col. Streight's ambush. "Old Forrest" formed his 300 best mounted men in a column of fours and ordered them to shoot to the right and left as they galloped through the half mile stretch of pines. A bugler sounded, "Charge!" and off they went, whooping, yelling and shooting. They rode so fast in the evening twilight that the Federal sharpshooters did not have time to aim properly and the Rebel losses were few. When the charge struck the low hill, the fight went rather badly for Col. Streight. His second-in-command and rear guard commander was killed by a carbine shot from Pvt. Joseph Martin, Company "I," Starnes' 4th regiment. Several others were also fatalities, and the men were demoralized. When the rest of the command caught up with Forrest at about 9 PM, Pvt. Whittsitt was told that Pvt. Hartwell Hunt, one of his dearest friends, had been killed in the skirmish.

Sgt. William R. Haynes of McLemore's regiment was captured and was questioned by Col. Streight. The young sergeant was so solemn and truthful in appearance that it seemed he could not lie about anything asked of him. The boys in his company called him "Parson" Haynes. When asked about the strength of Forrest's force, Sgt. Haynes carefully replied that besides his old brigade, which had been under the command of Col. Starnes, Forrest had Roddey's, Armstrong's and several others whose names he did not know. Streight probably did not take the sergeant's account as the gospel truth, but the intensity with which Forrest had pursued and fought him was reason enough not to totally disregard the captive's exaggerations.

Forrest sent a skeleton squadron to "bedevil" Streight's men of the Mule Brigade who were on their third all-night march in a row, wearily stumbling toward Rome, Georgia. The rest of the command was allowed to sleep for an all-night rest. During the night the harassing squadron got in front of Streight and set an ambush, which he thought was the main Rebel force, and he took a three-mile detour to avoid them. When he got to the Chattooga River, the ferryboat used by Capt. Russell, had been taken by the citizens. After wearily marching several miles, it was daylight when the crossing and burning of the old Dyke bridge was accomplished.   At 9 AM on Sunday, May 3, 1863, Streight's command stopped to rest near a few houses at a place called Lawrence in the "Straight Neck Precinct."

When the rested Rebels came up to the burned bridge near Gaylesville on the Chattooga River, they were ordered into the river on horseback. Although the stream was swollen from spring rain runoff, the cavalry got across by swimming their horses a few yards in the middle of it. There was some trouble getting the two guns over, but it was accomplished without much delay while the ammunition was transferred over the river by canoes that the citizens provided.

By 9 AM, Forrest's depleted command caught up with the hapless men in blue who had ridden all night and could no longer stay awake.   Col. Streight had   received a message from Capt. Russell, saying that he had arrived at the bridge over the Coosa to find it strongly defended by the Home Guards and Gov. Joseph E. Brown's Georgia Militiamen. Col. John Wisdom, the volunteer courier for Forrest, had outridden Capt. Russell, arrived in Rome, and gotten out the local troops. Russell did not think it advisable to attack with his two companies. He had also received information that a strong column of Confederate cavalry was on a parallel course and closer to Rome than was he. This force was Maj. Anderson with Col. Edmondson and his regiment. Col. Streight did not know that their orders were to keep him from swinging north and escaping across the Tennessee, rather than closing in and combining forces with Forrest to destroy him.

Forrest came up in a very noisy demonstration of officers giving commands for the movements of troops, that would lead even a veteran commander to the distinct impression that at least two brigades were moving into position. He deployed McLemore on his left flank, Biffle on the right, his escort and his brother's remaining scouts in the center of a crescent-shaped line around three sides of a wooded hill.   The trees masked the number of his men and guns as the skirmishers advanced in a noisy firing of rifles and pistols.

The Federal pickets were driven in, but neither the crackle of small arms fire nor the exertions of their officers could wake more than half of the exhausted men. When Streight ordered his awake men to lie down to present smaller targets, many fell asleep. His troops were literally asleep on their weapons in line of battle. Gen. Forrest sent Capt. Henry Pointer, of his staff, forward with a flag of truce to request surrender.

Col. Streight agreed to talk with Gen. Forrest to determine what terms he was being offered, if he surrendered his command.   Forrest demanded immediate surrender, "your men to be treated as prisoners of war; the officers to retain their side-arms and personal property." "Old Bedford" knew he had to convince Col. Streight, carefully and cautiously, that he had the men, guns and favorable position to certainly defeat him. If he brought on a pitched battle, outnumbered well over three to one, his command might well be destroyed. Forrest presented an air of confidence and indulged in gross exaggeration concerning his strength. Streight asked for twenty minutes to consult with his officers. Forrest needed time also. When he returned to his men, he ordered that the two guns be marched around the wooded knoll in a circle, to make it look as if two or three batteries were on the field.

Streight was opposed to surrender, but his officers voted unanimously to end the fighting. The Yankee colonel demanded that Forrest march his men out to show that he had a force equal to his own. Forrest refused and ordered his bugler, "Sound to mount." Streight agreed to surrender.

Pvt. W.H. Whittsitt described the surrender:

> Before ten o'clock in the morning we bore down upon the camp of the enemy and finding him unprepared for battle... and before noon the surrender had been accomplished. The place was crowded with undergrowth, and Streight proposed to march down the road until they found an open field suitable to the business of laying down their arms. Forrest gave assent, and in a few minutes we were in the road which shortly became a lane with immense fields of growing cotton on each side. That was the longest lane I have ever travelled. It may have been a mile, but it seemed ten miles in length. Streight had about fourteen hundred and fifty men, and we had about four hundred seventy-five in line. We were drawn upon both sides of them, and every man of them carried a loaded rifle and some likewise loaded pistols.

Whittsitt continues:

> If they had concluded to renew the struggle, it is difficult to understand how any of us could have escaped alive. Forrest galloped up and down the column and busily gave orders to couriers to ride to the rear and order imaginary regiments and batteries to stop and feed their animals and men. But the regiments of Starnes and Biffle and Ferrell's Battery, which had been depleted to skeleton proportions, were the only available troops within a hundred miles.
>
> Finally the lane came to an end, and there was a field of broom sage on the right-hand side. Col. Streight led the way and his troops were shortly formed in line. Then at the word of command they dismounted, stacked arms, remounted and rode away. There was an inexpressible sense of relief when they had parted company with their arms and ammunition...

Pvt. J.R. Harris, whose gun had failed to fire back in the spring of '61 when he aimed his first shot of the war at an enemy who had fired on him and missed, had a brief comment:

> I was in the chase after Streight [in his native Alabama], and when the surrender was made in front of Rome, Forrest had 434 men in line and Streight about 1,680; I think.

> Starnes' and Biffle's men,... did not venture to suggest the fewness of our numbers until we had delivered them safely to the keeping of the guards whom the [Confederate States] government had dispatched to Rome to receive them.

The victorious troops entered the city on the afternoon of May 3, 1863 to a royal welcome by the Georgian Romans. Streight's men said they were treated well by Forrest's men after their surrender, according to one of his sergeants, "... who have used us as a true soldier would treat a prisoner."

In a report to the Confederate States War Department in Richmond, Gen. Braxton Bragg summed up the success of the pursuit of the Federal expedition that had left Nashville April 10th:

> May 3, between Gadsden and Rome, after five days and nights of fighting, General Forrest captured Colonel Streight and his whole command, about 1,600 with rifles, horses, etc.

During the celebration of the saving of Rome, "our victory was embittered by a message that Stonewall Jackson had been wounded [by his own men] in a battle in Virginia" (Chancellorsville, May 2nd). Gen. Jackson died eight days later. The town was filled with refugees and 2,000 convalescents from army hospitals and had gone wild with excitement. Several of Starnes' men found some of their female kin and other relatives there. Soft pillows and feather beds with clean sheets were certainly welcomed after having slept on their saddles with a bedroll on the ground, when they had gotten a brief chance to sleep.

Capt. Russell, with tears in his eyes, had no choice but to surrender his two companies who had not been able to force a crossing of the Coosa. His men brought the number surrendered to about 1,600. Col. Edmondson and Maj. Anderson rode in with their regiment and joined the merriment. Now that they were prisoners, the townspeople offered their hospitality to Streight's raiders. The good Colonel remained glum over the ruse used to cause his surrender and declined any and all invitations to join the revelry.

Pvt. Dan Baird maintained that "Starnes' men were the bravest of the brave." According to Baird, they did not much fear to charge Yankee infantry who fired by volley or command.

Col. J.W. Starnes' well-trained men, without the presence of their ill commander and fighting under the second-in-command, Maj. W.L. McLemore, received the "Thanks of the Congress of the Confederate States of America:"

The thanks of the Congress are again due General N.B. Forrest and the officers and men of his command for meritorious services on the field, and especially for the daring skill and perseverance exhibited in the pursuit and capture of the largely superior forces of the enemy near Rome, Georgia.

A grand barbecue and feast were planned for Wednesday, May 6th, but on the night of the 5th, a courier rode in with intelligence that a large Federal force was advancing from Tuscumbia toward Talladega, Alabama. The boys were greatly disappointed to be ordered out for a forced march back to Gadsden, where they learned that Gen. Dodge was not advancing and had returned to Corinth, Mississippi.   Col. Biffle took charge of the return, a detachment picked up the wounded men and abandoned supplies along the way.   Gen. Forrest went to see Gen. Bragg.

Back at cavalry headquarters at Spring Hill, Col. Starnes was having some difficulty in recuperating from what was probably a severe case of influenza. He was still too ill to reorganize his depleted brigade from those who, themselves or their horses, had given out in the pursuit of Streight's raiders and were straggling into camp.   At this time the cavalry corps commander, Gen. Earl Van Dorn, was seen on occasion riding about in his buggy in the company of the attractive, young wife of Dr. George Peters, a local physician, who was almost certainly an acquaintance of Col. Starnes during the days of his medical practice.

While Col. Starnes was in Spring Hill awaiting the return of his victorious troops, Dr. George B. Peters saw his wife riding to parade with Gen. Van Dorn. Shortly thereafter, on the morning of May 8, 1863, he killed the small, elegant General with a pistol shot in the back. Dr. Peters stated that Van Dorn had "violated the sanctity of his home." Van Dorn's friends denied there was any affair going on between Mrs. Peters and the general. They claimed that the shooting was in cold blood for political reasons.

Gen. Forrest was promoted to the command of the cavalry corps to replace Van Dorn. He arrived back at Spring Hill on May 16th. Confederate Secretary of War, James A. Seddon, wired Bragg the next day to send Forrest or some other cavalry force to Mississippi.   The Confederate government considered the situation there rather desperate. Grant had run past the batteries at Vicksburg and landed his army south of the city. In a bold operation, Grant moved out, living off the land, without a line of communication, and had been defeating Gen. Pemberton's scattered Confederate divisions in detail at Jackson, Champion's Hill and the Big Black River. "Red" Jackson's division and Roddey's brigade were rushed to

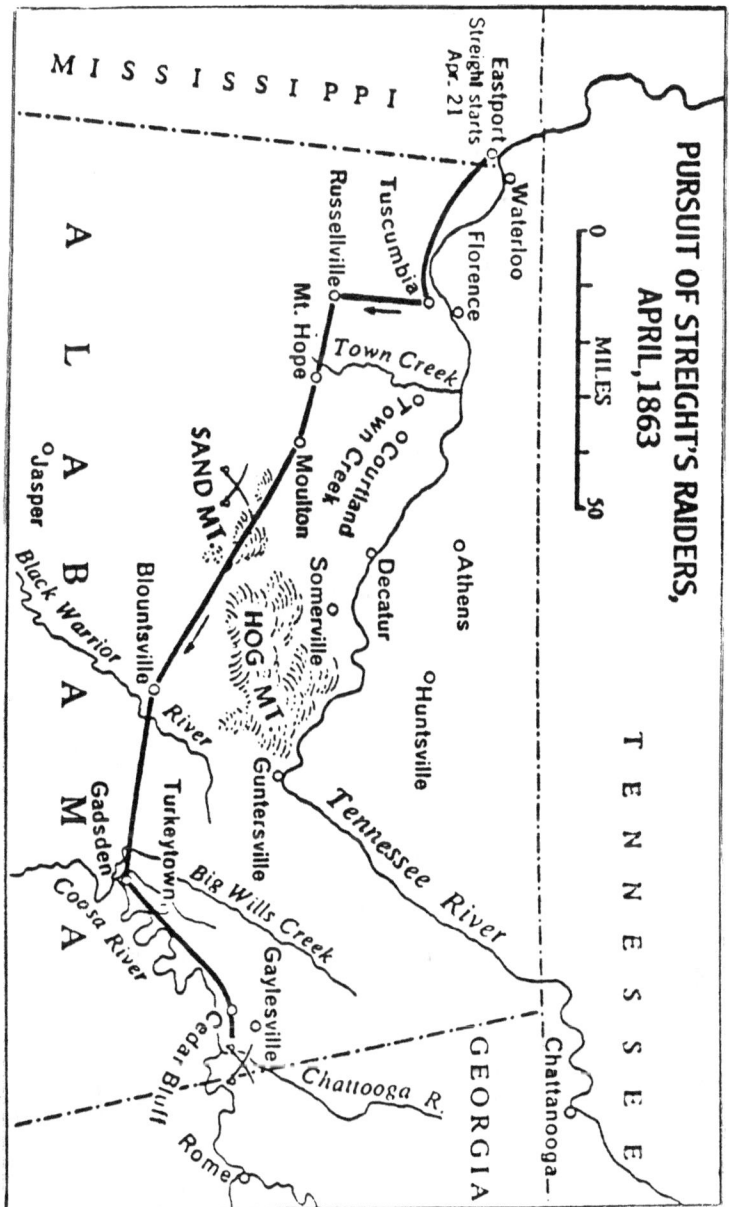

PURSUIT OF STREIGHT'S RAIDERS, APRIL, 1863

MISSISSIPPI

ALABAMA

TENNESSEE

GEORGIA

Eastport
Streight starts
Apr. 21
Waterloo
Florence
Tuscumbia
Russellville
Mt. Hope
Town Creek
Courtland
SAND MT.
Moulton
Town Creek
Decatur
Athens
Jasper
Somerville
Huntsville
HOG MT.
Blountsville
Black Warrior River
Guntersville
Tennessee River
Gadsden
Turkeytown
Big Wills Creek
Coosa River
Gaylesville
Cedar Bluff
Chattooga R.
Rome
Chattanooga

0   MILES   50

From Wyeth, Life of General Nathan Bedford Forrest, 1899

Williamson County

Mississippi. This left Forrest with only the two small brigades of Starnes and Armstrong to guard the whole left wing of Bragg's Army .

There was daily action at one or the other outposts, but nothing of significance occurred during the last two weeks of May. Col. Starnes returned to his command and was again on scout and picket duty, with his cavalry brigade, in the area of his family plantations and former medical practice, between Spring Hill and Columbia to the south, and Franklin and Triune farther north. During the first week in June, Gen. Forrest learned that Gen. Granger had moved his Federal headquarters to Triune, almost halfway to Murfreesboro from his former position, and only five miles or so from the Starnes' plantation. The small Confederate cavalry division then set out on June 4th to determine the Union strength still posted in Franklin.

Forrest marched up the Columbia Pike with Starnes at the head of his brigade. He dispatched Armstrong and his brigade on the Lewisburg Pike. About three miles from Franklin, on both the Columbia and Lewisburg Pikes, Federal pickets were encountered. Col. Starnes chased the pickets into town and his men made a number of captures. By using the houses to shield his troopers, Starnes charged right into the heart of his hometown.

Gen. Forrest was riding with Starnes when he saw the waving of white flags. Col. John P. Baird of the 85th Indiana Infantry, commanding the post, had begun an urgent call for help and was using signal flags to contact Gen. Granger in Triune. The Confederate commander ordered Starnes to cease firing and rode forward with an attendant, likewise displaying an emblem of truce, with the intention of having an interview with Col. Baird and hopefully negotiating a surrender. Before he had gone very far, a Union officer called out to him from behind a hedge, " General Forrest, you will retire at once. This is no truce. That is a signal flag." The officer had been captured by Forrest at Murfreesboro almost a year earlier and had been treated courteously as a prisoner of war.

The two guns of Morton's battery that had accompanied Starnes' brigade were unhitched from their horses and rolled up Main Street by hand, while shelling the Union troops in the houses and the fort. Starnes was able to take possession of the town, with the exception of the loopholed houses immediately under the protection of the garrison and Fort Granger on the bluff on the north side of the Harpeth River. They were able to hold the place long enough to batter down the Williamson County Jail doors and release all the prisoners. Starnes' troopers emptied the sutler and commissary stores into impressed wagons and sent them out toward Spring Hill.

Starnes did not have a particularly difficult time in taking Franklin or in determining Federal strength still posted there. Things were not going so well with Frank Armstrong, who had been posted out on the east side of the town in the direction of Triune. Gen. Granger, in response to Col. J.P. Baird's signals for for help, hurriedly dispatched the 1st Cavalry Brigade, under Col. Archibald P. Campbell, to the relief of Franklin. This fine brigade was composed of the 2nd Michigan, 4th and 6th Kentucky and 9th Pennsylvania.

Just before sundown they dashed into Armstrong's brigade a mile and a half from the town. Armstrong had advanced Col. T.G. Woodward's battalion and five companies of the 1st Tennessee Cavalry out on the road to Triune. Much to his chagrin, he had not brought up the remainder of the brigade, which was still on the south side of the Big Harpeth. Armstrong fought stubbornly with the troops he had in the hope of effecting a safe withdrawal. The Federal cavalry vigorously pushed his men back to within sight of the river. In sharp skirmishing with the 2nd Michigan and 6th Kentucky, Gen. Armstrong, his bodyguard and battle flag were captured. Armstrong managed to escape a little later, but his battle flag and men who were taken prisoner remained in the custody of Gen. Granger's cavalry.

Col. Baird and Gen. Granger reported that Franklin was being attacked by, "three brigades, under Forrest, Armstrong and Starnes." Col. Amson W. Hobson, upon hearing the brisk firing, advanced hurriedly to reinforce Armstrong with his 3rd Arkansas cavalry regiment, and was successful in covering his retreat across the Harpeth. Forrest and Starnes heard the heavy firing and noticed that the sounds of the musketry were drifting south, meaning that Armstrong was being driven back across the stream. They feared that a strong enemy force might be getting between Starnes' brigade in Franklin and their base in Spring Hill. The brigade was immediately withdrawn from the town and soon joined Gen. Armstrong. By this time it was dark, and both brigades went into camp for the night in line of battle, three miles from the river in the direction of Spring Hill.

The Confederates retired the next day, June 5th, to their base encampment at Spring Hill. The Federal commanders made no attempt to follow them. Col. Campbell reported that if he could have had another hour of daylight, he could have taken Armstrong's whole command, but that the night was so dark that it was impossible to follow them. Gen. Granger reported fifteen Confederates killed and wounded and eighteen captured from Armstrong's brigade.

This, the third Williamson County courthouse, was completed in 1858. The four columns are cast iron. During the Civil War it was used as Federal headquarters

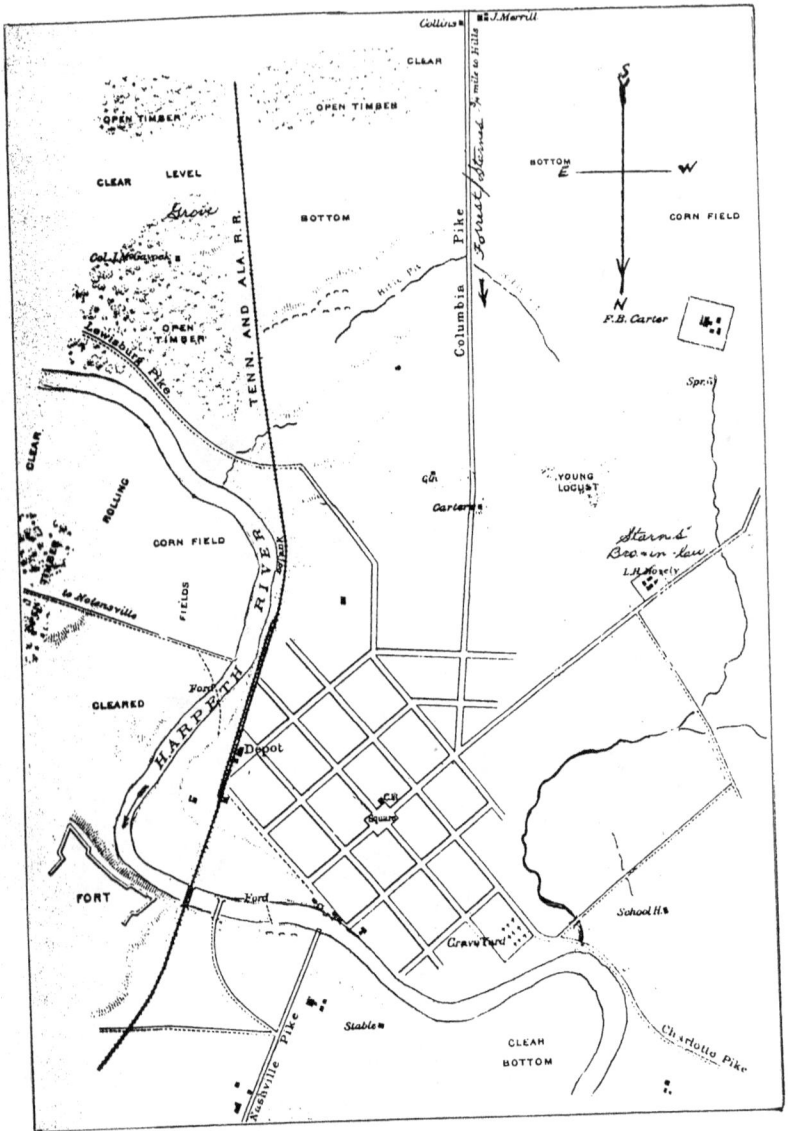

**Forrest's Attack on Franklin, Tennessee, June 4th 1863,
with Starnes' Cavalry Brigade**

The Tullahoma Campaign

On June 9th, Gen. Bragg ordered Forrest to make a forced reconnaissance on the Federal position in Triune. The next morning, he moved out with Starnes' and Armstrong's brigades and the Georgia regiments of Avery and Crews. The whole division was on the march toward Triune up the Chapel Hill Road, with the exception of those posted on the heavy picket line Forrest had ordered. Col. Starnes crossed the Harpeth with his brigade near the settlement of College Grove, only three miles or so from the Rudder plantation his wife had inherited from her father.

They drove the 1st Tennessee (Union) Cavalry pell-mell into town as they approached and began shelling the breastworks. All the Yankees on the front took cover behind the breastworks. But, on observing only cavalry on the field, the Federal infantry moved out in force and pushed back Starnes' and Armstrong's men. Two cavalry brigades under Col. Campbell and Brig. Gen. Robert B. Mitchell attempted to get on the right and left flanks and to the rear of the Confederate cavalry. Skirmishing briskly, Forrest's small division retreated rapidly in good order and recrossed the Harpeth.

When the Federals were driven in behind their works, Gen. Forrest ordered his brother, Maj. Jeffery Forrest, to drive off the herd of fine beef cattle that was grazing in a nearby field. The successful capture of the beef animals was the principal accomplishment of the expedition. Gen. Mitchell said, "Being without artillery, and the enemy having such an advance, I did not deem it advisable to follow them further." Union losses were reported as four killed, eighteen wounded and six missing. Forrest made no report of losses that appears in the records.

At considerable risk from Federal patrols, Col. Starnes made occasional visits, usually at night, to see his expectant wife at their home on the south side of the Harpeth. Now that his promotion to Brigadier General was anticipated, he and Mary Christina searched the house for any goldware pieces she had hidden away from the ransacking troops of either army who might happen by Rudderville. They were trying to locate enough gold to mold a general's star for his collar badge. Since early March Starnes had been commanding "Forrest's Old Brigade," the 2nd Brigade of Forrest's Division.

As early as June 1st, Forrest relayed information to Gen. Bragg that Starnes' scouts had reported a concentration of Union cavalry in front of Gen. Rosecrans' army at Murfreesboro, and expressed his opinion that they were "going to move forward or backward." This gave Bragg three weeks advance notice, but he was surprised and caught off guard on the 22nd by the massive Federal advance. He was without proper intelligence or alternative plans. Gen. Bragg ordered Forrest to withdraw his picket lines and to retreat via Shelbyville to Tullahoma.

Spring Hill, June 23, 1863 - 7 a. m.

Major-General Wheeler:
        my command present is composed of three regiments; effective strength, 1,100. Shall cooking utensils and ambulances be taken? I am ready to move at a moments notice.

J. W. Starnes

Colonel, Commanding Brigade

Again, as was the case before the Battle of Stone's River, when the Confederate authorities weakened the Army of Tennessee by transferring forces to Mississippi, Rosecrans, as soon as he heard of these moves, began an advance.   A Federal feint was made toward the entrenchments at Shelbyville, but the heavy columns were sent through Liberty Gap, Hoover's Gap and Matt's Hollow. These moves turned the Confederate right flank. Bragg's Chief of Cavalry, Gen. Joseph Wheeler, held Guy's Gap on the Murfreesboro-Shelbyville Road. Forrest was ordered to meet him at Shelbyville.

Starnes assembled his brigade near Triune and camped at College Grove the night of June 26th. All the scouts were ordered to report in before midnight. To coordinate his march with that of Gen. Forrest and Armstrong's brigade, he moved out at 1 AM and did not halt, on this 30-mile ride, until reaching the vicinity of Shelbyville. Here he found that the advance units of the Union Army were already in the town in large numbers. The Colonel then ordered a turnabout and retraced the line of march until he came to the road that led toward Sims' Bridge across the Duck River.

Maj. T.F.P. Allison rode back to where he found nineteen-year-old Sgt. Thomas R. Tulloss in the column, and said that the Colonel wanted to see him at once and to bring his faithful, old, Negro man, Blunt. The young kinsman of the Colonel found him at the junction of the roads. Col. Starnes said that he had promised his wife that if it looked to him like the army was going out of Tennessee, he would send for her and carry her with him. He added that she had not been well for some time (she was well into her seventh month of pregnancy with their fifth child) and may not be well enough to make the trip. The Sergeant said that Mrs. Starnes might prefer some older man to conduct her trip, but the Colonel quickly advised him that they had discussed the matter thoroughly, and she wanted Sgt. Tulloss to see that she was driven out. There were no horses left at his home, the Colonel said, and asked if Blunt could not hitch up the horses they were riding to the barouche and drive them as a team.

Tulloss and his man, Blunt, rode most of the night, then stopped in a wheat field, fed their horses on the wheat and slept in a fence corner. The Sergeant was never to see Col. Starnes again.

Country Store built by Dr. J.W. Starnes at Rudderville, TN in the mid-1850's

An antebellum house on the former Starnes/Rudder estate, where Mary C. Rudder Starnes was said to have spent her last days

After a ride from Spring Hill without incident, on that afternoon of the 27th, the rest of Forrest's division reached the vicinity of Shelbyville between five and six o'clock. There they found that Wheeler's cavalry had been pushed across the Duck River by massed Union cavalry, and with the wagon trains across, were ready to fire the bridge. Maj. G.V. Rambaut, of Forrest's staff, rode up and reported that his commander was within sight of Shelbyville and advancing rapidly to secure a river crossing.

Wheeler quickly recrossed the bridge with Brig. Gen. W.T. Martin and about five hundred of his men with two pieces of artillery. They had scarcely reached the other side when they were charged by the Federal cavalry, in a column of fours, who ran right over them. In the confusion a caisson was overturned and the Confederate cavalry dispersed. Seeing the retreat blocked, Gen. Wheeler, urging his men to follow, jumped his horse off a fifteen-foot riverbank and into the stream. The Yankees were so surprised that they did not immediately take advantage of the situation. Wheeler, Martin and many others made it across, but an estimated forty to fifty of their men were shot or drowned.

Meanwhile, Armstrong and Forrest, also finding the town of Shelbyville filled with Union soldiers, swung around four miles east to cross the Duck River on another bridge. They got to the rear of the army to protect the Confederate train as it moved slowly in the rain and axle-deep mud toward Tullahoma. Martin's division was temporarily demoralized and disorganized. That night Gen. Gordon Granger missed an opportunity, only nine miles away, to fall upon Bragg's enormous train of unprotected, floundering wagons. There was not an organized and effective unit between Gen. Granger's Union forces and the train. Maj. Gen. D.S. Stanley proposed following the Confederate withdrawal during the night, but his request was not approved by his superior. Gen. Granger reported:

> Forrest passed around our rear last night, moving eastward, had I known..., I could have thrown my force between the retreating army and his forces.

By late Sunday morning of June 28th, Forrest's cavalry division had caught up with the main body of the army at Tullahoma. There was not nearly enough cavalry to cover the Confederate flanks and screen the front. Bragg had acceded to Brig. Gen. John H. Morgan's repeated requests to conduct another raid into Kentucky with 2,000 men as recently as June 18th. Morgan's popularity and reputation, were failing in the opinion of both the military and citizens. He needed a boost to his ego, via a flamboyant expedition, after his headquarters in McMinnville had been overrun by Federals in late April. His wife was captured, and he barely escaped, himself. Since the May transfer of Jackson's and Roddey's cavalry to Mississippi, Bragg now had less than 9,000 left of the 16,000 he had had in the spring. Rosecrans now had 12,000 mounted infantry and cavalry at his command.

While Gen. Forrest raced to the rear with Armstrong's Brigade to protect the bridges threatened by Federal cavalry, Col. Starnes and his brigade were ordered posted on the Manchester Pike. Here he encountered the advance units of Rosecrans' Army and characteristically assailed the Federal force to determine its strength. Starnes threw a heavy skirmish line forward in the early afternoon, and a very lively firing developed at Bobo's Crossroads about five miles northeast of Tullahoma, out on the Old Hillsborough and Lynchburg Road.

The 1st and 3rd divisions of the Federal XIV Corps had reached Manchester by midnight on the 27th. At 2 PM the next afternoon, they started out in the direction of Tullahoma and set up camp at Crumpton's Creek. Col. Ferdinand Van Derveer's 3rd Infantry Brigade (of Brig. Gen. John M. Brannan's 3rd Division from Maj. Gen. George H. Thomas' XIV Corps) threw out a strong advance one and a half to two miles to their front. This advance encountered Starnes' dismounted cavalry pickets and began driving them back as the firing intensified. Col. Starnes rode out to encourage his small brigade to hold their ground and to look for a spot to place a battery. He was accompanied by Capt. Daniel F. Wade, Company "C," of the 3rd (Clack's) Tennessee Infantry, who was still recovering from a severe wound received at Fort Donelson and had preceded his regiment's transfer from Mississippi to Gen. Bragg's Army. Capt. Wade, a fellow Williamson County resident from the Spring Hill area, was dressed in his best gray uniform with all the braid and insignia of his rank. Starnes wore a neat, plain uniform as he rode across the muddy fields.

The Federals extended their lines around the Confederate left, and the range became even shorter for the Union sharpshooters. Capt. A.W. Hubbard, of "E" Company of Starnes' old 4th regiment, and several others expressed their concern for the colonel's safety and asked him to please go to the rear, out of rifle range. He politely thanked them for their consideration, but remained near the front.

Nearby, Pvt. Ben F. Martin of Capt. Hubbard's company, a neighbor of the Starnes', had found a small patch of good, ripe whortleberries and was picking and eating them between the skirmish lines. Pvt. Frank Overall, Company "C," 4th Tennessee Cavalry, also a Starnes neighbor back in Williamson County, was close by in the line of skirmishers, as was that "good old boy from Alabama," Pvt. J.R. Harris. Capt. Wade suggested to Col. Starnes that they retire, since the Federal sharpshooters were beginning to get them in range. Starnes, like his commanding officer, Nathan Bedford Forrest, was brave to a fault. He politely responded to Wade that he could move toward the rear if he were concerned for their safety, but he, himself, would remain in the forward position. Capt. Wade was as brave as any Confederate officer on the field and declined the offer. The troopers thought that their brigade commander was preparing to retire from the front, but he lingered under a large tree, studying the situation.

Only a few minutes later, around 3 PM, a bullet from a sharpshooter's rifle struck Col. Starnes in the side at the waist, passed through a kidney and out the front on the other side. Wade, slightly to the rear of Starnes, rode forward, grasped the reins of both their horses in his left hand, supported the Colonel with his right arm, and made it to the Confederate infantry picket line of the 48th Tennessee. There Wade fainted from the pain of the unhealed wound in his right hip, and both officers fell from their horses. The 48th's troops thought both had been killed. When Wade revived, the infantrymen were dipping up rainwater with their hands from the wagon wheel ruts in the field, and pouring it in his face. Capt. Henry G. Evans of the 48th, said that Col. Starnes was brought to his lines and placed on a litter in the road. He also said that a Negro sharpshooter was credited with the shot that mortally wounded Col. Starnes.

Pvt. J.M. Jackson, "a plain, old, unassuming Tennessean," said that he just happened to see the puff of smoke from the sharpshooter's gun when the fatal shot was fired. Keeping some treetops between them, he made his way to within about fifty yards of the sharpshooter's tree. Jackson then shot him from his perch, the body, "falling like an ox" to the ground. He procured the man's Whitworth rifle and took it away with him.

In early 1863 the Confederates imported the first twelve of these English, muzzle-loading rifles with an 1800-yard effective range, hexagonal bore and telescopic sights. Six were given to Lee's Army of Northern Virginia; the others went to Bragg's army in the west. If Pvt. Jackson was correct in identifying the rifle as a Whitworth that was used to mortally wound Col. Starnes, it was likely the first, or one of the very first, to be captured and employed by a Union sharpshooter. Pvt. Jackson of Company "I," Starnes' 4th Cavalry, had his moment as a hero with the men and officers for his quick avenging of "General Starnes'" death.

That evening, Sunday, June 28, 1863, as Col. Starnes lay mortally wounded, Sgt. Tulloss and Blunt rode up to the Starnes home at Rudderville. They found Mary Christina Starnes "fast in bed." She asked to consult with the Sergeant's father about the advisability of her trying to go to the Colonel but, of course, was not aware that her husband had been mortally wounded a few hours earlier. Sgt. Tulloss went home and sent his father, John Ebenezer Tulloss, a former sheriff of the county, to see Mrs. Starnes. John Tulloss was the Colonel's first cousin and was also the same age. They talked and decided she was not able to make the trip. Young Tulloss promised Mrs. Starnes that he would come for her as soon as she was able to travel, and he and Blunt left at once for the front.

During the night of Monday, June 29th, Gen. Bragg told Capt. Wade to stay with Col. Starnes until he died; surrender, tell Gen. Rosecrans the circumstances, bury the Colonel and ask for exchange or parole. Starnes lived thirty-six hours after having been wounded. Bragg first decided to fight and then to withdraw, as the Federals continued flanking his position at Tullahoma.

On the 29th, Union Gen. George H. Thomas reported to Brig. Gen. James A. Garfield, Rosecrans' Chief of Staff, from Manchester:

A brigade from the Third Division was thrown forward on the Tullahoma road... Col. Starnes, of the Confederate cavalry, reported among the killed. The road from Manchester to this point was rendered nearly impassable by one of the strongest and steadiest rains ever experienced.

His later report stated, "The rebel General Starnes reported among the number killed."

Dr. Watson Meredith (known as "Dr. W.M.") Gentry, an old friend, attended Col. Starnes and was with him when he expired. This surgeon from the 17th Tennessee Infantry then notified Mrs. Starnes.

When Col. Starnes died at about 3 AM, June 30, 1863, a Confederate, A.Y. Smith, said, "his body was brought to our house," in Tullahoma. Capt. Wade took an ambulance as a hearse and, early in the morning, drove through the streets of Tullahoma followed by a funeral cortege of retreating soldiery. Lt. Broomfield L. Ridely was riding up the street to report as an aid to Maj. Gen. A.P. Stewart and stopped to inquire. He was told it was the body of Col. J.W. Starnes who had been shot at the head of his command in a hot skirmish a few miles out.

Wade drove rapidly to Winchester, some fifteen miles to the south. There he bought an expensive coffin and hired some Negroes to dig a grave. Pvts. Joseph E. Couch, Phillip M. "Bud" Westbrook and two others from Starnes' original Company "F" volunteered as an honor guard and pallbearer detail. While the grave was being dug, it was reported that the Federals were coming. The grave was hurriedly filled. Col. Starnes would have been 46 years old on July 9th. Wade escaped capture and reported to Gen. Bragg.

The men of his old 4th Cavalry command, in their soldierly grief, reflected on the death of their commander, whom Gen. Forrest had selected to command his "Old Brigade." Pvt. W.H. Whittsitt said, "His loss is deeply deplored, and his name is revered by all those who appreciate courage and capacity."

Marshall Thompson, the Colonel's eleven-year-old "personal valet," sighed:

Don't know how they got him, but I knows he was a chargin when it happened... the Cunnel was a powerful brave man.

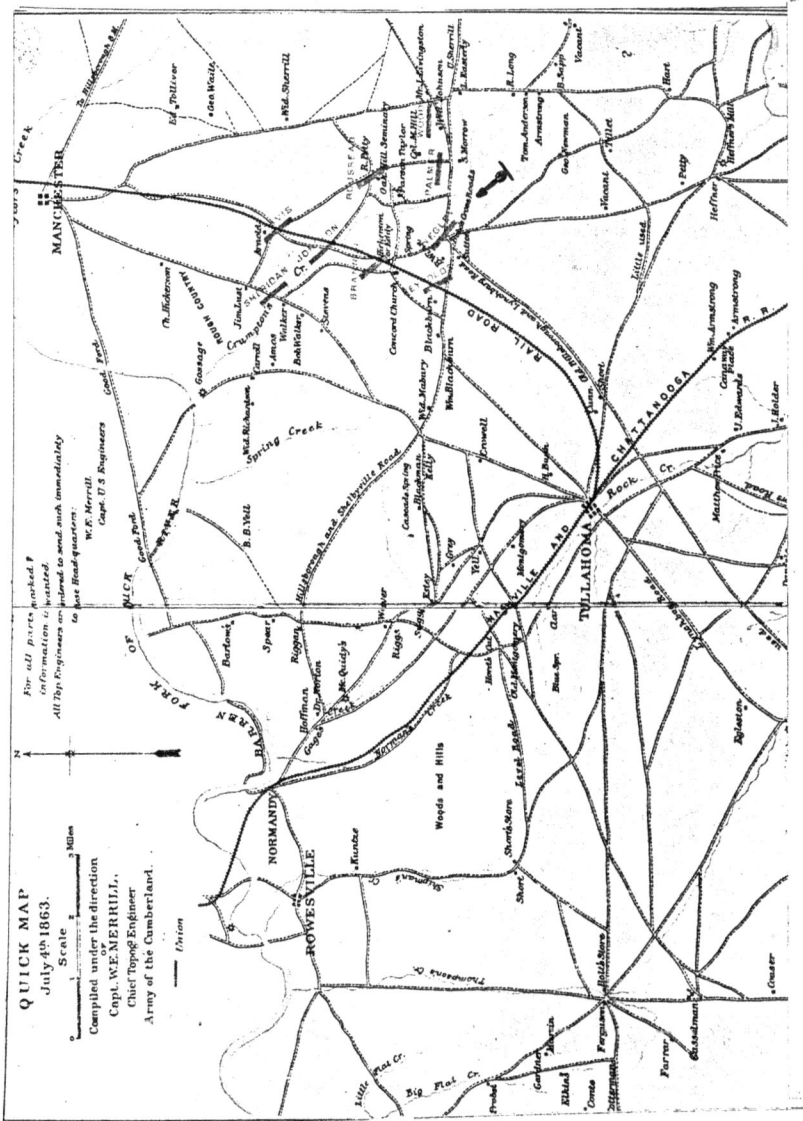

The arrow indicates the position of Starnes' Cavalry Brigade at Bobo's Crossroads when Col. Starnes was mortally wounded by a Union sniper June 28, 1863

The contrast in personalities and styles of command between the educated, small-statured Col. Starnes and the large-figured military genius of his unlettered friend and commander, Gen. Forrest, was not lost on the men. After he saw the polite and gentlemanly colonel mortally wounded, Pvt. J.R. Harris summed it up in a brief bit of eloquence: "*He was a kind hearted man, and could lead brave men farther than most men, while Forrest could make a coward fight.*"

Capt. Thomas W. Davis, 1st Tennessee Cavalry, expressed the mood of the southern soldier in his diary during this period of the struggle in constant downpours, deep mud and nearly impossible movement of men and equipment: "July 1st Wednesday; General Bragg moved Quarters... I figured he was going to retreat. I feel despondent. Col. Starnes is dead."

Despite her state of illness and advanced pregnancy, Mary Christina Starnes made her way to the Colonel's brigade encampment near Tullahoma. Dr. Gentry did everything possible to make her comfortable and to help the others who knew her well in their efforts of consolation. James Patton, an old neighbor and friend, was present and had marked the grave site.

Col. Starnes' passing came at the time the death knell of the cause was being sounded all across the Confederacy. Lee lost the July 1st - 3rd Battle of Gettysburg in the north, Pemberton was preparing to surrender the yet undefeated, but starving, garrison to Grant at Vicksburg in the west, and Bragg was now in full retreat toward Chattanooga in the Confederate middle section.

Col. George Dibrell assumed command of Forrest's old brigade on July 1, 1863. Major W.S. McLemore was promoted to Colonel, commanding the 4th Tennessee Cavalry Regiment, and it became known as "McLemore's."

When the body of Pvt. Marcus L. Martin, "E" Company, 48th Tennessee Infantry, killed in the Battle of Chickamauga, was brought home for burial in Williamson County, a newspaper clipping was found in his pocket that appeared to be an editorial, by the typeface, from the Tuesday, July 2, 1863 Chattanooga *Daily Rebel* :

Col. James Starnes - *Only a few days ago we were urging the claims of this gallant officer for the commission of Brigadier General. With sensations of the most profound regret, in which the people of Tennessee will join with one heart, we announce his fall at the head of his troops in the van of battle. He was mortally wounded while on reconnaissance duty on Sunday afternoon by one of the enemy's sharpshooters. The wound was in the bowels, and after lingering for thirty-six hours, he died night before last.*

For many months Col. Starnes has commanded a brigade of cavalry under Forrest, and with success. He gave early promise of distinction in the character of the most dashing partisan leader of Middle Tennessee. During the woeful summer of 1862, and throughout what will be known in history as the 'Guerrilla Campaign,' he commanded a crack regiment of mounted men, and spread terror into the ranks of the enemy under Buell, right under the guns of the interior camps and fortifications. At this period his fame rivaled that of Morgan.

Many of his exploits are wholly unrecorded and numbers of them forgotten amid the confused turmoil of war, and its crowded canvass of events. After the most useful career as an independent commander, Col. Starnes was attached to the regular cavalry service, and has gained a rare, though not noisy reputation in the service for courage reliability and skill.

Personally he was a man of unblemished character as a Christian and citizen. His manners were quiet and reserved, but respectful and kind. He was in the prime of life, and the vigor of experience. The tears of a bereaved family and the sorrow of a devoted band of comrades follow him to an early but hallowed grave. All honor his name.

The End

Reinterment site of Col. James W. Starnes
Rudder-Starnes Cemetery
Williamson County Tennessee

Sites and Dates of Starnes' Principal Skirmishes and Engagements

Dec. 28, 1861 Sacramento, KY
Apr. 10, 1862 Wartrace, TN
June 7, 1862 Readyville, TN
Aug. 30, 1862 Richmond, KY
Sept. 3, 1862 Frankfort, KY
Nov. 5, 1862 Nashville, TN
Dec. 18, 1862 Lexington, TN
Dec. 20, 1862 Humboldt, TN

Dec. 31, 1862 Parker's Crossroads, TN
Feb. 3, 1863 Fort Donelson, TN
Mar. 5, 1863 Thompson's Station, TN
Mar. 25, 1863 Brentwood, TN
Apr. 10, 1863 Franklin, TN
Apr. 30, 1863 Sand Mountain, AL
June 4, 1863 Franklin, TN
June 28, 1863 Tullahoma, TN

Epilogue

The Regiment and Brigade

After Col. Starnes' death, his old 4th Tennessee Cavalry Regiment, McLemore's, and his former 2nd Brigade, Dibrell's (temporarily under Col. Nicholas N. Cox), continued to cover Gen. Bragg's withdrawal from Tullahoma to Chattanooga. From there they were involved in picket and scouting operations as the Federal army moved on that river and rail center. Bragg decided to evacuate Chattanooga on Sept. 6, 1863, and the cavalry brigade became involved in the complicated maneuvers of both opposing armies in the mountainous region of lower east Tennessee and north Georgia, until the Battle of Chickamauga.

No specific report of the 4th Cavalry Regiment's participation in this battle has been found, but the reliable Pvt. William H. Whittsitt recounted the story of Forrest's men involved as infantry in heavy fighting on the extreme right of the Confederate line on Sept. 19 and 20, 1863. The long-standing disagreements between Bragg and Forrest finally reached a climax, and on the 28th. Forrest was ordered to turn over his command to Gen. Wheeler.

The regiment and brigade went with Wheeler's cavalry in support of Lt. Gen. James Longstreet's attempt to retake Knoxville in mid November. They continued to operate in east Tennessee in the early part of 1864, but were back with the Army of Tennessee near Dalton, Georgia by late April under Col. Dibrell. In the meantime Gen. Bragg had been relieved by Gen. Joseph E. Johnston on February 24, 1864.

As part of Gen. Wheeler's cavalry, McLemore's regiment and Dibrell's brigade participated in the Atlanta Campaign from Dalton to Atlanta. There Gen. Joseph E. Johnston was relieved of command of the Army and was succeeded by Gen. John B. Hood on July 17, 1864.

Assigned the mission of destroying the railroads between Maj. Gen. William T. Sherman's armies around Atlanta and their base of supply at Nashville, Wheeler set out on a sweeping raid on August 10th northward through Georgia and into Tennessee. Dibrell was left at Sparta, Tennessee on September 2nd to recruit in his home territory. While attempting to rejoin Wheeler's corps, he was attacked between Readyville and Woodbury.

Unable to break through, he turned into east Tennessee and southwest Virginia. This caused the 4th Tennessee to be split between the six companies, with Dibrell and four companies remaining with Col. McLemore in Wheeler's corps. In the Battle of Saltville, Virginia on October 2,1864, Col. Dibrell reported that his command consisted of his old 8th, six companies of the 4th (McLemore's) and Col. Paul Anderson's 4th Tennessee regiments. They rejoined Wheeler for the Savannah Campaign of November and December.

After the fall of Atlanta, Forrest began his raid into northern Alabama and central Tennessee from Tupelo, Mississippi on September 16, 1864, to begin a planned attempt to disrupt Sherman's communications north of the Tennessee River. On the 24th he met with Wheeler, who turned over to Gen. Forrest "what he has of my old brigade," Biffle's, Nixon's and McLemore's (four companies) very severely depleted regiments. Those troops remained with Forrest through the end of the year. On January 20, 1865 at Verona, Mississippi, Gen. Forrest ordered Holman's, DeMoss', Biffle's and Russell's regiments retained, and sent back Wheeler's and the 4th Tennessee, and all other parts of regiments and detachments whose commands might be in Georgia. Presumably Col. McLemore and the four companies joined Dibrell in South Carolina.

Col. Dibrell was promoted to Brigadier General, C.S.A on January 28,1865. After Gen. Lee's surrender on April 9,1865, Dibrell was sent from Gen. Johnston's Army in Raleigh, North Carolina to President Davis at Greensboro. Gen. Dibrell commanded about 2,000 cavalrymen as escorts for the Confederate president. Col. McLemore commanded the few remanents of Dibrell's old brigade in the escort detachment. The Federals intercepted the President's party at the Savannah River, and Mr. Davis continued on with an escort of about sixty men.

The Confederate train was carrying an estimated $108,300 from the C.S.A. Treasury, which was distributed to the men in the sum of about $25 each in specie. Starnes'/Dibrell's brigade colors were not surrendered. The brigade color-bearer, Pvt. Elbert J. Peacock, Company "E," of Starnes' old 4th Tennessee Cavalry Regiment, cut up the colors and gave pieces of it to some ten or twelve of McLemore's couriers and staff officers. Dibrell surrendered his escort cavalry division at Washington, Georgia on May 7, 1865.

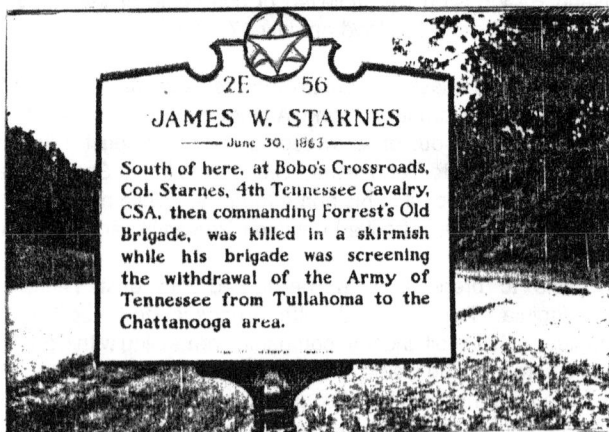

Tennessee Historical Commission Marker on Highway 55, about halfway between Manchester and Tullahoma

There are two basic European immigrant origins of the old southern U.S. family surname, Starnes. They are the 1630 Stearns family's arrival in Massachusetts from Suffolk County, England, and the 1710 Staring family entry into New York from the German Palatinate. Both of these family lines have played very colorful, participating roles in the colonial and early U.S. history. Col. James W. Starnes was a descendent of the English Stearns line who changed the spelling of their name after having migrated southward in the Colonies.

Isaac Stearns and his wife, Mary, emigrated to Watertown, Massachusetts in the year 1630 aboard the "Arabula" (or Arabella), which also carried Governor Winthrop from Suffolk County, England. It is generally accepted that two of his brothers, Daniel and Shubael, accompanied Isaac on the voyage. Shubael died shortly after having arrived in the New England colony and Isaac raised his two orphaned sons, Charles and Nathaniel.

Charles Stearns, born ca. 1625, lived in Lynn, Massachusetts and married Rebecca Gibson (his second wife) from Cambridge in June of 1654. They named their firstborn Shubael II, born September 20, 1655. In 1681 Shubael II married Mary Upton of Reading, Massachusetts.

Shubael III was born in 1683; his brothers were named Samuel and John. He married Rebecca Larriford (some references show Larriby) on December 28, 1704 in Saco or Kittery, Maine (then a part of Massachusetts). Their son, Shubael IV, born January 28, 1706 in Boston, was later to become an early Baptist minister. They also had three other sons and six daughters: Peter, Isaac and Ebenezer, Rebecca, Elizabeth, Sarah, Hannah, Mary and Martha.

Shubael III became town clerk in Tolland, Connecticut, and some of his descendants say that he began to sign his name as "Starnes" as early as the 1720's. Another family tradition states that Shubael IV first used the Starnes spelling in Tolland in 1752, shortly after his ordainment.

About 1745 Shubael IV joined the "New Lights" religious movement which originated with the ministry of George Whitfield. These churches were converted, New England, congregational communities who believed in immersion as the baptism of the New Testament. He was baptized by immersion in the spring of 1751 by the Rev. Whit Palmer in Tolland, and on May 20th of that year was ordained as a Baptist minister.

Feeling there was much to be accomplished in his ministry outside New England, the Rev. Shubael Stearns, his wife, Sarah, and others of his family, migrated southward in 1754. A descendent of this family group, wrote in 1835 that they "had the view of spreading the gospel to the Mississippi River." With Shubael IV were his brothers, Peter and wife, Hannah Stinson, Ebenezer and wife, Ann, his sisters, Martha and husband, Daniel Marshall,

Rebecca and husband, Jonathan Polk, Elizabeth and husband, Enos Stinson. Shubael IV and Sarah had no children, but the several children of the others were with them.

For a time they stopped on Opequon Creek in Northern Virginia near the settlement of Winchester. There was already an established church at this place with a pastor and a meetinghouse. After a brief stay the Stearns group moved on south to arrive at Sandy Creek, North Carolina on November 22, 1755. The Rev. Shubael and his companions, numbering sixteen, constituted the first church congregation there in Guilford (now Randolph) County, 20 miles southeast of Greensboro, and four miles west of Liberty, North Carolina. A 26' X 30' meetinghouse was built in 1762. The log meetinghouse, built in 1802, still stands on the site. Rev. Stearns died in 1771 and is buried near the church.

Peter Starns, the brother of the Rev. Shubael Stearns, and wife, Hannah, had four sons and three daughters. The sons were Charles, Ebenezer, Levi and Joel. Rhoda Starns McGraw and Thamar Starns Free were two of the daughters. Peter settled with his kin along the Broad River in South Carolina. His wife, Hannah (a cousin), died in Tablas Fort near Augusta, Georgia before the Revolutionary War. He remarried and fathered sons, Joshua and Peter, by his second wife.

Isaac, the third brother, had but one child, Hephzibah Starnes. She married William Wellborn and bore him ten sons and four daughters.

Ebenezer Starns first married the daughter of David Callahan and had a daughter, Elizabeth, and son, Moses. She died of cholera morbus and he then married Elizabeth Young. Samuel Scott Starnes, Daniel, John Hadley, Ebenezer and Mary were born of this second marriage. They all were living in Augusta, Georgia in 1808.

Daniel Starnes, a printer by profession, operated a book store and published a paper called "The Mirror of the Times." Daniel, in partners with his brothers, drew up partitions, obtained subscribers and established the first stage line to run from Columbia, South Carolina to Augusta, Georgia, and from there to Milledgeville, then the state capital.

Upon the death of Daniel, Dr. Samuel Scott Starnes, born July 4, 1786, sold out the business, and married Nancy Matilda Wellborn, his second cousin, the granddaughter of Hephzibah Starnes Wellborn, in 1816. There had been an understanding between the four brothers and one sister that they would find an appropriate, desirable place away from Augusta and settle there for the rest of their lives. They searched the country for about two years. After the birth of Dr. Samuel and Nancy's first child, James Wellborn Starnes, in Wilkes County, North Carolina on July 9, 1817, Samuel, John and Mary E., who had married Capt. Rhodon Tulloss on November 22, 1808, moved to Williamson

County, Tennessee. Ebenezer joined them later. John H. soon married Miss Jane Ware.

Note: The above Stearns/ Starnes direct descendent, paternal lineage is underlined, and the direct maternal lineage double underlined for Col. James Wellborn Starnes.

Dr. Samuel Starnes (d. 1841) and Nancy Matilda Starnes' (d. 1842) children were: James Wellborn (b. 7/9/1817, d. 6/30/1863), Mary Adeline (b. 6/8/1820), Shubael (b. 1/15/1823, d. 4/27/1846), Elizabeth Rebecca (b. 11/6/1826), Catherine Maria (b. 1/9/1829), Nancy Parthenia (b. 8/2/1831), Samuel Scott, Jr. (b. 7/9/1835), John Daniel (b. 7/4/1837) and Ebenezer (b. 1/24/1840 d. 4/10/1863).

Daniel Starnes died when a young man. His children, Ebenezer, Camilla and Augusta, were raised principally by Dr. Samuel Starnes.

John Hadley Starnes was the father of seven children, four of whom died young. Those who reached maturity were: Mary Elizabeth (b. Oct. 5, 1822), Samuel W. (b. Feb. 20, 1829) and Camilla Augusta (b. July 20, 1836).

Ebenezer Starnes had two sons and two daughters: William A., Sarah, Ebenezer and Mary.

Mary E. Starnes Tulloss (8/23/1790 - 11/14/1840) had eleven children, three of whom died young. The living were: Maria Y. (b. 2/4/1810), Louisa E. (b. 3/29/1812), Samuel Starnes (b. July 9, 1815), John Ebenezer (b. 11/30/1817), Ann M.W. (b. 3/26/1820), Robert C. (b. 6/7/1822), Mary Jane (b. 10/2, 1824) and Joshua (b. 5/12/1827).

Dr. James Wellborn Starnes married Mary Christina Rudder (1830 - 1904) on April 19, 1849. Their children were: Cora D. (4/7/1850 - 5/9/1859), Henry M. (11/12/1851 - 1/19/1859), James W., Jr. (7/10/1853 - 2/16/1894), Marian B. (12/12/1860 - 8/19/1863) and William Rudder (8/10/1863 - 8/7/1895).

Sons, James W. Starnes, Jr. and William Rudder Starnes, were the only children of Colonel James W. Starnes to survive childhood. William R. married Viola C. Reppard in Savannah, Georgia in 1886 and was the father of James W. and Mary C. Starnes' only grandchildren, Reppard R. and Wellborn M. Starnes. James Jr. was never married and was said to have been killed in a railroad accident.

William Rudder Starnes and his aunt, Parthenia Starnes (1) Tulloss (2) McCord, operated a mule breeding and trading business. When she died, "Parth" left to him her half of the Rudderville mule business and the sum of $10,000.

Reppard Rudder Starnes (born Jan. 24, 1887 in Williamson County, Tennessee, died Mar. 3, 1958 in Battle Creek, Michigan) was one of the children chosen, whose grandfathers had done the most for the Confederacy's war effort, to dedicate the Confederate monument in Franklin, Tennessee.   Reppard R. attended the Battleground Academy in Franklin, Tennessee, the Sewanee Military Academy in Sewanee, Tennessee, Vanderbilt University and the University of Virginia. He enlisted in the army the day after the US entered WWI, and completed a course in one of the war's first officer's training schools.   Reppard was discharged as a Captain at Camp Custer, Battle Creek, Michigan in August of 1919.

Reppard married Elizabeth F. Bruckner in Detroit on Aug. 14, 1920. Their children were a daughter, Frances V., and sons, Reppard A. and Robert W. Reppard R. Starnes was a real estate broker and furniture dealer for many years, and very active as an officer of his local American Legion Post.

> Frances Violet Starnes (5/9/22-9/89) married William Schultz.

> Reppard Anthony Starnes (1/17/24) married Helen Rozenkovich in 1955. Their children are: Mary T., born 1957, married Brian Wunderlind; Susan K., born 1959, married Charles Sennertt; Constance A., born 1961, married Paul Clark; William R., born 1963.

> Robert William Starnes (11/2/27) married Margery Boothroyd on 7/15/50; their children are: Robert D., born 6/20/51, married Cynthia; Carol B. (5/29/54-6/12/57), James Richard, born 1/21/56, married Cynthia Leonard; Deborah S.,born 4/17/58; Laura J., born 3/15/60, married William Wylie; Virginia Lou, born 7/28/63, married Stephen Taylor.

Wellborn McCord Starnes (1891-1964) married Alice Cohen (1894 - 1948) on November 10, 1914 in Nashville, Tennessee. Wellborn also served in the US Army during WWI and was discharged with the rank of captain.   Their only child, Mary Catherine Starnes (b. 1917), married Thomas M. DeMoss, Jr. (1914-1985) on November 10, 1937. (Thos. M. DeMoss II was the great-grandnephew of Lt. Col. Wm. E. DeMoss who served in Col. Jas. W. Starnes' cavalry brigade). Their children are:

> Thomas M. DeMoss III (b. June 1, 1950) married Sandra Chambers in 1973. The children are: James, Julie and Davis.

> Mary Alice DeMoss (b. March 17, 1954).

Family Portraits

The Starnes family portraits were originally painted in 1858 by Washington Cooper.

In 1878 Mary Christina Rudder Starnes commissioned artist George Drury to repaint her portrait from the earlier original.

According to Wellborn M. Starnes, his grandmother then had the original portrait of herself destroyed.

In 1992 Mary Catherine Starnes DeMoss, great-granddaughter of James W. and Mary C. Starnes, had the family portraits restored.

Mary C. Starnes DeMoss

Dr. James Wellborn Starnes (July 9, 1817 - June 30, 1863)

Mary Christina Rudder Starnes (1830 -1904)

Cora D. (April 7, 1850 - May 9, 1859), Henry M. (Nov. 12, 1851 - Jan. 19, 1859) & James W., Jr. (July 10, 1853 - Feb. 16, 1894) Starnes

Andrews, J. Cutler, The South Reports The Civil War. Princeton, NJ: Princeton University Press, 1970.

Baird (Beard), Dan W., "With Forrest In West Tennessee," Southern Historical Society Papers (1909).

_____,"Forrest's Men Rank with Bravest of the Brave," Southern Historical Society Papers (1909).

Boatner, Mark M., The Civil War Dictionary. New York: David McKay Co., Inc., 1959.

Catton, Bruce, Never Call Retreat. Garden City, NY: Doubleday & Co., 1965.

Davis, Burke, The Civil War: Strange & Fascinating Facts. New York: Fairfax Press, 1962.

DeMoss, Mary Starnes, correspondence with the author (6/26/86 to 5/19/94).

Fuqua, Tom, Rutherford's Confederates March Again As Seven Gray Veterans Answer Mess Call (Sept. 19 publication). Mufreesboro, TN.

_____, "Starnes' Pussonal Valet Tells of the Years Under Forrest," Nashville Tennessean (June 11,1933).

Gray, H.T., "Forrest's First Cavalry Fight," Confederate Veteran (March, 1907).

Harris, J.R., "First Shot Fired on Alabama Soil," Confederate Veteran (July, 1901).

Henderson, J.H., "Gallant Capt. Samuel L. Freeman," Confederate Veteran (June, 1911).

Henry, Robert Selph, First With the Most, Forrest. New York: Bobbs-Merrill Co., 1944.

Kennerly, O. Dan, The Dawn of Lightning War. Houston: Parkers Crossroads Press, 1992.

"Last Roll, The; Samuel P. Claybrooke," Confederate Veteran (May, 1910).

Lytle, Andrew N., Bedford Forrest and his Critter Company. Seminole, FL: Green Key Press, 1984.

Mathes, Capt. J. Harvey, <u>General Forrest,</u> in <u>Great Commanders</u> series. New
    York: D. Appleton & Co., 1902.

Morris, Roy, Jr., "Battle in the Bluegrass," <u>Civil War Times Illustrated</u>
    (December, 1988).

Nolen, C.L., "Dibrell's Old Flag Not Surrendered," <u>Confederate Veteran</u>
    (November, 1906).

O. R. <u>The War of the Rebellion: A Compilation of the Official Records of the</u>
    <u>Union and Confederate Armies.</u> Series I: Vol. VII, Vol. X, Pt.1, Vol.
    XVI, Pts. 1 & 2, Vol. XVII, Pt. 1. Vol. XX, Pt. 1, Vol. XXIII, Pt.1, Vol.
    LII Supplement, Pt. 1; Series II, Vol. V.

Porter, James D., <u>Tennessee</u> Confederate Publishing Company,1889.

Ridley, B.L., "Chat with Colonel Wm. S. McLemore," <u>Confederate Veteran</u>
    (June, 1900).

Smith, Franklin H., <u>Frank H. Smith's History of Maury County, Tennessee,</u>
    published interviews, (1904-1908).

Starnes, John H.* genealogical letter (1855).

Starnes, Robert W.** letter to the author (August 2, 1994).

<u>Tennesseans In the Civil War</u>, Parts I & II Nashville: Civil War Centennial
    Commission of Tennessee, 1965.

Tulloss, Thomas R.*** "Battle of Douglass' Church," from the collection of
    personal, historical papers of Susie Gentry.

_____, <u>History of Col. James W. Starnes of Williamson County</u>
    (Publication No. 22) Williamson County Historical Society, Spring
    1991.

_____, "When Capt. Sam Freeman Was Killed," <u>Confederate</u>
    <u>Veteran</u> (August, 1913).

---

* Family genealogical letter written to his nephew Judge Ebenezer Starnes in Atlanta,
transmitting and updating a copy of a letter written by his brother, Dr. Samuel S.
Starnes , Sept. 6, 1835 to their older half-brother, Moses Starnes, in Mississippi.

** Great-grandson of Col. James W. Starnes.

*** Includes the official report of Col. James W. Starnes.

Whittsitt, W.H., "A Year With Forrest," Confederate Veteran (August, 1917).

"Whitworth Rifle Sharpshooters," Confederate Veteran (August, 1894 and April, 1908).

Witherspoon, J.G., "The Killing of Captain Freeman," Confederate Veteran (August, 1913).

Williams, Steve A., "Charge Both Ways: The Battle of Parker's Crossroads," Confederate Veteran (September, 1985).

Wyeth, John A., That Devil Forrest. New York : Harper & Row, 1959.

_____ , Life of General Nathan Bedford Forrest, New York: Harper and Bros., 1899.